Contents

Technology is best when it brings people together.

— Matt Mullenweg

1. Embarking on a Journey into the Deep

Imagine a world beneath the waves, where the mysteries of the universe unfold not among the stars but in the dark, uncharted caverns of alien oceans. This book will take you on an astounding journey into the realm of cybernetic cephalopods—a visionary blend of biology and technology that redefines intelligence in ways humans have only begun to explore. These remarkable creatures, nestled in their oceanic worlds, illuminate the boundless possibilities of both nature and machine working in harmony.

Explore the genesis of their existence, the intricacy of their cybernetic enhancements, and the far-reaching implications of their intelligence, not only on their own ecosystems but also on our understanding of life and consciousness. With each chapter, you will delve deeper into the intriguing qualities that allow these augmented beings to thrive in their alien oceans. Be prepared to challenge your perceptions and expand your horizons as you uncover the secrets of cybernetic cephalopods and their reign beneath the waves.

2. Genesis of the Cyber-Cephalopod

2.1. The Origins of Cephalopod Intelligence

The capability for complex intelligence found in cephalopods represents a remarkable confluence of evolutionary history and environmental adaptation. This intelligence did not arise overnight; instead, it is the product of millions of years of evolution, woven through the intricate tapestry of marine ecosystems. To truly appreciate the origins of cephalopod intelligence, one must examine their evolutionary pathways, environmental contexts, and the unique adaptations that have equipped them for survival in diverse and often challenging underwater arenas.

Cephalopods belong to the class Mollusca, a highly diverse group of organisms known for their soft bodies and, in many cases, protective external shells. Early cephalopods, such as the ammonites, evolved hundreds of millions of years ago and exhibited primitive forms of intelligence characterized by basic behaviors such as camouflage and predation strategies. However, the lineage that we recognize as modern cephalopods—encompassing octopuses, squids, and cuttlefish—began to display more sophisticated cognitive abilities. This shift in cognitive complexity can largely be attributed to their unique environmental challenges and predatory lifestyles that necessitated advanced problem-solving skills.

The transition from a predatory lifestyle to one characterized by both predation and evasion set the stage for the development of complex social interactions and enhanced problem-solving capabilities. Cephalopods have evolved to occupy various niches in marine ecosystems, manipulating their environments with remarkable dexterity. They do not rely solely on brute force; instead, they employ strategic thinking and adaptability, utilizing their ability to change color and texture to blend in seamlessly with their surroundings, a testament to their intelligence in both evasion and hunting.

Neuroscientific analyses reveal that cephalopods possess a distributed nervous system with a significant portion of their neurons located in their arms rather than solely in their brains. This decentralized arrangement allows for autonomous motor function and sensory perception, suggesting a unique form of intelligence that enables them to process and respond to various stimuli effectively. The unique neuroanatomy of cephalopods contributes to their high levels of cognitive function, including learning and memory skills. Recognizing patterns and solving problems are crucial in their interaction with the complex environments of the ocean.

Learning is another area where cephalopod intelligence shines. Experimentation and observation have demonstrated their ability to learn from experience and adapt their behaviors accordingly. For instance, octopuses have showcased problem-solving abilities in laboratory settings, successfully navigating mazes or opening jars to retrieve food—a clear indication of cognitive flexibility. Moreover, studies have shown that cephalopods can retain learned behaviors, suggesting a level of memory that allows them to recall and utilize previously acquired information in new contexts, an essential trait in the wild where they must constantly navigate changing environments and challenges.

The social structures present among certain species of cephalopods further attest to their complex intelligence. While many cephalopods are solitary hunters, some exhibit social behaviors that include signaling, communication, and even cooperative hunting strategies. Cuttlefish and squids, for instance, have shown the capacity to engage in complex visual displays that may enhance group cohesion or serve as warnings to potential threats. Such behaviors necessitate an understanding of the social dynamics at play, which points to the sophistication of their cognitive abilities.

Moreover, evolutionary pressures have driven innovation in cephalopod intelligence. The oceans, particularly those in which cephalopods thrive, present unpredictable challenges and changing dynamics. Competition for resources, predation, and environmental shifts have all played substantial roles in sculpting the cognitive landscape of these creatures. The offspring of intelligent ancestors had better survival odds, leading to the perpetuation of traits such as memory and adaptability across generations.

The introduction of cybernetic enhancements marks an era of unprecedented evolution in cephalopod intelligence. By augmenting their existing cognitive frameworks through complex technologies, the potential for enhanced cognitive capabilities rises dramatically. The confluence of organic neurobiology and technological interface opens a new frontier, accelerating the evolutionary trajectory beyond what we once believed possible. This merging of the biological and the technological not only holds the potential to deepen the understanding of intelligence but raises profound questions about the essence of consciousness itself.

In summary, the intelligence of cephalopods is a remarkable product of their evolutionary history, characterized by their environmental adaptations, decentralized nervous system, learning abilities, and complex social behaviors. It reflects a unique blend of survival instincts and cognitive capacity, positioning cephalopods as one of the ocean's most enthralling creatures. As we continue to explore the intersections between their inherent intelligence and the enhancements brought about through technology, we uncover deeper insights into the nature of intelligence—both biological and artificial—and its implications for the future of life beneath the waves.

2.2. The Advent of Cybernetic Integration

The early phases of cybernetic integration were marked by breakthroughs in understanding both the biological underpinnings of cephalopod physiology and the potential of technology to augment that biology. Researchers commenced their journey with a series of daring experiments, driven by the desire to merge cephalopod natural talents with advanced technology. Initially viewed with skepticism, these ambitions began to find footing in the minds of enthusiastic scientists and engineers, who believed that both the mysteries of cephalopod intelligence and the growing field of cybernetics could be intertwined to explore entirely new avenues of intelligence and interaction.

The foundational work in this revolutionary field stemmed from a comprehensive decoding of the cephalopod nervous system. Scientists recognized that these creatures possess a unique neuroarchitecture, with an impressive proportion of neurons not confined to the centralized brain but dispersed throughout their arms. This decentralized design presented fertile ground for developing cybernetic interfaces that could directly interact with biological systems, leading researchers to envision cybernetic enhancements that could amplify the cephalopod's innate abilities—intelligence, problem-solving, dexterity, and perception—while respecting the living essence of these fascinating beings.

The initial steps toward cybernetic integration involved the application of biocompatible materials designed to interface seamlessly with the cephalopod's biology. Researchers experimented with various polymers and metals that could withstand the underwater environment while allowing for the absorption and exchange of neural signals. Such developments laid the groundwork for implants that could facilitate communication between the cephalopod's nervous system and the augmentative technologies that would later evolve into sophisticated enhancements.

As researchers refined their techniques, the first successful integrations unfolded in controlled settings. Cybernetic enhancements began with sensory augmentations—technologies designed to heighten the natural capabilities of cephalopods in detecting environmental stimuli. Devices were created that integrated seamlessly with the cephalopod's existing sensory organs, allowing for enhanced vision, including the capacity for wavelength detection beyond normal ranges. This not only empowered cephalopods with significantly improved echolocation abilities but also provided them with an expanded understanding of their immediate surroundings, pushing the boundaries of their natural perceptual world.

Subsequently, efforts turned towards enhancing motor skills. Robotic extensions mimicking the flexibility and movement of cephalopod appendages were developed. These extensions allowed for increased dexterity and strength, enabling cephalopods to manipulate objects with precision far beyond what was achievable through their biological arms alone. Initial prototypes of these enhancements underwent rigorous testing in both laboratory settings and natural environments to assess their impact on the cephalopod's behavior, with remarkable results. Cephalopods equipped with cybernetic tentacles were not only capable of executing tasks faster but began to display innovative problem-solving capabilities that prompted fascination and further inquiry into the potential of these enhanced creatures.

However, the partnership between biology and technology was not merely one of enhancement; it was a dialogue. The cephalopods themselves contributed to the evolution of this integrated system. Researchers noticed that as they introduced increasingly advanced cybernetic features, cephalopods adapted their behaviors to incorporate and leverage these new capabilities. They began to experiment with their enhancements, testing limits and establishing unique interaction patterns with their environments that researchers had not anticipated. This dynamic interplay signified a transformational phase; the amalgamation of biology and technology was not a one-way street but rather a symbiotic relationship leading to enhanced intelligence and adaptability.

This era of experimentation also experimented with the integration of artificial intelligence systems, which played a crucial role in enhancing elusiveness and tactical thinking. Computer systems were developed that could analyze the rapidly changing marine environment, providing real-time feedback to the cephalopods. This allowed the creatures to make informed decisions, adapting their strategies based on dynamic stimuli—be it the presence of potential predators or changes in resource availability. The emergence of AI-equipped cephalopods opened new frontiers in understanding not just animal intelligence but also the emergent properties of intelligence itself, merging organic cognition with machine-based processing.

Despite the exhilarating possibilities, the introduction of cybernetic integration faced numerous challenges and hurdles. Questions regarding the ethics of enhancement surfaced, discussions arose about the potential loss of cephalopod identity, and concerns about the implications of manipulating lives for research and experimentation began to swirl around the scientific community. It became clear that with great possibilities came great responsibilities. This prompted reflective dialogue within the interdisciplinary domains involving marine biologists, ethicists, engineers, and technology specialists, igniting debates about where the line should be drawn in the enhancement of living creatures.

Overall, the advent of cybernetic integration within cephalopods illustrated a fascinating intersection of biology and technology that not only raised profound questions about intelligence and existence but also carved pathways for new explorations within our understanding of life beneath the waves. As researchers continued their ambitious explorations into this alien territory, the promise that cybernetic cephalopods would illuminate not just their own existence, but also humanity's relationship with intelligence and consciousness, seemed brighter than ever. The oceanic world, once veiled in mystery, began to reveal its secrets, propelled forward by the union of flesh and technology, fostering a new age of understanding and discovery hidden in the depths.

2.3. Biological and Mechanical Symbiosis

The synthesis between biological cephalopod features and mechanical enhancements encapsulates a remarkable evolution of life beneath the waves. This confluence of organic and artificial elements can be understood through a multidimensional lens, examining the intricate mechanics behind the interactions of flesh and machine, and the profound consequences that arise from this partnership for both the cybernetic cephalopods and their environments.

At the core of biological and mechanical symbiosis is the notion of interdependence—where biological instincts and capabilities are significantly augmented by technological advancements. Cephalopods, known for their extraordinary adaptability and intelligence, provide a unique foundation for this integration. Their natural abilities, from

11

advanced camouflage to dexterous manipulation of objects, form the biological canvas onto which mechanical enhancements are infused.

Researchers and engineers began to observe that augmenting cephalopods' existing traits could yield a higher degree of functionality for survival and adaptation to complex underwater environments. Consider the example of enhanced vision. The eyes of cephalopods are already marvels of nature, capable of perceiving a wide spectrum of colors, even in the dim light of deep oceans. By integrating cybernetic sensors, scientists extended their capacities, allowing them to detect bioluminescent signals and identify even subtle changes in water composition. This advancement not only amplified their hunting acumen but also refined their navigation skills, transforming how they interact with their surroundings.

Mechanical enhancements also extend to physical attributes, like the tentacles, key instruments for gathering sustenance and interacting with their habitat. The introduction of robotic appendages modeled on the flexibility and strength of natural cephalopod limbs permits a level of control and precision previously unattainable. Equipped with enhanced sensory feedback, these mechanical arms can perform intricate tasks, reclaim food more efficiently, and navigate within intricate environments with greater ease. Such advancements illustrate how cephalopods adapt to leverage these enhancements creatively, leading to increased independence and problem-solving skills that showcase their cognitive prowess.

However, the intersection of biology and technology is not merely additive; it is transformative. The interplay between organic cephalopod behaviors and mechanical functions generates new paradigms of intelligence and interaction. As cephalopods began to integrate their enhancements, their behaviors morphed, leading to unexpected capabilities. They started experimenting with their new appendages, finding novel ways to interact with their environments and develop unique strategies for evasion, hunting, and social communication. This not only enriched their survival strategies but also fostered a unique evolutionary path, seemingly accelerating their cognitive evolution in response to the enhancements.

One poignant area of exploration stems from the cephalopods' neural architecture and how it interacts with mechanical upgrades. With a significant portion of their neural makeup located in their limbs, the introduction of cybernetic elements facilitates a direct communication pathway between biological and electronic systems. This allows the cephalopods to maintain their sophisticated reflexive responses while incorporating computational processing effortlessly. As a result, cephalopods equipped with these cybernetics can execute rapid decision-making, like evasive maneuvers or tactical offensive strategies, based on processing vast amounts of real-time data, including sensory input and environmental context.

This enhanced interactivity also prompts fascinating implications for how these cybernic cephalopods communicate with one another. By merging biological communicative signals, such as color changes and body postures, with digital interfaces, they can transmit information instantaneously, sharing knowledge about potential threats, food sources, or environmental changes. This creates a complex network of knowledge-sharing that transcends simple survival tactics, engendering a more rich social fabric among these creatures.

However, as beneficial as these integrations are, they also raise significant questions and challenges, particularly concerning the nature of identity and autonomy. While mechanical enhancements can substantially improve capabilities, they inevitably shift the fundamental essence of cephalopod existence. It beckons a dialogue about the nature of intelligence itself—does enhanced capacity equate to a more advanced form of consciousness, or does it dilute the very identity that defines these beings? This philosophical query permeates discussions among scientists, ethicists, and researchers, leading to a burgeoning discourse on the ethical implications of such enhancements.

Furthermore, the environmental ramifications of biological and mechanical symbiosis must be considered. These enhanced cephalopods are not merely living tools; they emerge as active agents capable of influencing their ecosystems. Their newly acquired skills can alter predatory dynamics, affect food webs, and modify interactions among marine species. The enhanced capabilities, while advantageous for the cephalopods themselves, could result in unforeseen consequences for the delicate balance of marine biodiversity.

Ultimately, the synthesis of organic and mechanical features in cephalopods epitomizes a pioneering frontier in evolutionary biology. It creates a living laboratory for exploring the complex intricacies of life, intelligence, and interaction in the natural world. As we deepen our understanding of these remarkable creatures and their cybernetic enhancements, we are not merely charting new technological territories but also reshaping our perceptions of intelligence, consciousness, and the essence of life itself beneath the ocean's surface. The journey of biological and mechanical symbiosis invites humanity to reconsider the future of interaction with our natural environment, paving the way for a holistic understanding of coexistence in an increasingly integrated world.

2.4. Ethics of Enhancement

The enhancement of natural organisms, particularly the cybernetic cephalopods in this exploration, presents a plethora of ethical considerations and debates that reverberate across multiple disciplines. As we push the boundaries of biological enhancement, it becomes essential to interrogate the implications of these technologies, evaluating their potential benefits and risks—not only for the cyborg creatures themselves but also for the human species and broader ecosystems in which they exist.

From a foundational perspective, the ethics of enhancement centers on the notion of consent and the autonomy of the enhanced organisms. Unlike traditional evolutionary processes, which unfold over extensive time frames and within natural selection parameters, the enhancements introduced to cephalopods occur at a pace and scale that raises questions of choice and agency. When researchers and engineers affix technological augmentations onto these marine beings, is there an inherent disregard for the innate qualities that define their uniqueness? It compels us to consider whether these enhancements, however beneficial they may seem, infringe upon the autonomy of the cephalopods—an autonomy that in nature allows for survival and adaptation outside human influence.

In considering the moral obligations towards these enhanced beings, we must delve into the implications of identity. What does it mean for a cephalopod, centrally defined by its extraordinary natural capabilities, to incorporate artificial enhancements into its biological framework? There is a risk that the introduction of cybernetic elements may dilute their biological essence, leading to an identity crisis that not only affects individual organisms but may also reverberate through populations and ecosystems. The risk of creating a new caste system among cephalopods—where enhanced individuals experience an elevated status over their unenhanced counterparts—fuels conversations about equity in the natural world.

Furthermore, the ethical landscape of enhancement stretches into the realm of environmental impact. The introduction of cyber-cephalopods with advanced capabilities could significantly alter marine ecosystems. Enhanced hunting prowess or superior adaptability may lead to cascading effects across the food web—putting pressure on both predator and prey species. The repercussions of elevating individual species through technological means could undermine the ecological balance that has evolved over eons. Such dilemmas urge us to probe into our responsibilities as stewards of marine life, our role in conservation efforts, and the long-term viability of biodiversity amidst our interventions.

As we traverse deeper into the complex ethical terrain of enhancement, the debate surrounding the purpose of these augmentations emerges as a focal point. The motivations behind cybernetic enhancements pose significant questions about human intentions. Are these enhancements primarily being driven by scientific curiosity and the desire for knowledge, or do they serve more anthropocentric purposes such as military applications, commercial gain, or spectacle? The potential for militarization of intelligent cephalopods equipped with advanced combat capabilities raises profound moral concerns concerning the exploitation of living beings—transforming them into tools for human advantage rather than recognition of their intrinsic value.

Moreover, there is the question of unpredictability. With the integration of technology, there arises an inevitability in variability of outcomes—some of which may defy our capacity to manage or predict. Cybernetic enhancements could lead to unforeseen behavioral changes in cephalopods or unanticipated interactions with their environments, complicating our understanding and control over their biological and ecological systems. The concept of precautionary measures becomes paramount; we are compelled to consider the risks of unintended consequences as we venture forth with biotechnological modifications.

In navigating these complexities, the collaborative ethos among interdisciplinary thinkers becomes essential. Engaging ethicists, marine biologists, engineers, and policymakers in open dialogue fosters a holistic understanding of the potentialities and dangers involved in enhancing natural organisms. Through meaningful discussion and discourse, we can establish ethical frameworks that embrace caution, responsibility, and respect towards cephalopods and their habitats, while still pursuing the innovative research that drives enhancement technologies.

The future of ethical considerations in enhancement will be defined by our understanding of responsible stewardship, respect for the natural order, and recognition of organisms as beings with their rights, not just instruments for human progress. As we delve into this new age of cybernetic exploration and possibility, we must tread with conscientiousness. By fostering a deeper awareness of the ethical dimensions of enhancement, we can navigate these uncharted waters with a shared commitment to ensuring that the power of technology uplifts, rather than diminishes, the living tapestry of life beneath the waves. The dialogue on ethics will serve as our compass, guiding us through the uncertain currents of enhancement toward a future where technology harmonizes with the natural world rather than disrupts its delicate balance.

2.5. Pioneers of Possibility

In the realm of pioneering cybernetic integration, several scientists and engineers stand as beacons of innovation, charting uncharted waters in the synthesis of biology and technology. These individuals have dedicated their lives to unraveling the complexities of the cephalopod's natural capabilities and enhancing them through cutting-edge cybernetics. Their work not only sheds light on the intricate mechanics of these incredible beings but also raises profound questions about the future of intelligence and our understanding of the consciousness that emerges from such remarkable unions.

One of the foremost figures in this field is Dr. Amina Khatri, a marine biologist whose fascination with cephalopods began during her youth, inspired by the elusive octopus. Holding a Ph.D. in neurobiology, Dr. Khatri first honed her understanding of cephalopod neural systems, investigating the distributed nature of their nervous systems. Her path intersected with the world of engineering when she began collaborating with technologists to explore gestures of communication between biological and artificial systems. Dr. Khatri spearheaded the development of biocompatible materials, crucial for the successful integration of cybernetic enhancements that would harmonize with cephalopod biology. Under her guidance, the first prototypes for sensory augmentations were born, enhancing the creatures' abilities to perceive their environment in unimaginable ways.

Dr. Khatri's work set the stage for pivotal technological breakthroughs, culminating in the development of an advanced neural interface known as the CephNeuroLink. This innovative device allows for real-time brain-computer interaction, enabling cephalopods to send and receive information, fostering not only enhanced problem-solving capabilities but also the capacity to integrate learned experiences from their interactions with their environments. Through careful observation and persistent experimentation, Dr. Khatri and her team have established new behavioral patterns in these cybernetic cephalopods, illuminating pathways for future generations of underwater exploration.

Equally influential in this sphere is Professor Lawrence Takeda, an engineer specializing in robotics. Professor Takeda's pioneering work in biomimetic robotics has been instrumental in creating advanced appendage technologies. His fascination with cephalopod locomotion led him to analyze the physical dynamics at play within octopus and cuttlefish movements. Working in tandem with marine biologists, he produced designs for cybernetic tentacles that replicate the flexibility, dexterity, and strength of natural cephalopod limbs. These enhancements not only empower cephalopods to navigate through complex marine terrains but also facilitate intricate interaction with their surroundings, fostering problem-solving skills that unlock new realms of intelligence.

The collaborations between Dr. Khatri and Professor Takeda, marrying biology with engineering, have orchestrated a flourishing environment for discovering the interdependence between living organisms and technology. Their collective research explores not just the mechanics of augmentation but also the evolutionary implications of integrating intelligence from diverse realms. They lead conversations around co-evolution, where both cephalopods and their enhancements evolve symbiotically, promoting cognitive capabilities beyond previous limitations.

Another critical voice in this dialogue is Dr. Ines Morales, a computer scientist focused on artificial intelligence applications in marine biology. Her vision has vastly contributed to understanding how cybernetics can enhance not only the sensory and motor functions of cephalopods but also their cognitive capacities through AI-infused systems. By implementing neural networks capable of analyzing vast amounts of environmental data in real-time, Dr. Morales has unlocked pathways for cephalopods to learn, adapt, and evolve their behaviors based on their ever-changing surroundings. Her AI-enhanced systems effectively communicate with cephalopod neural networks, resulting in a synergy that fosters an expanded understanding of the oceanic world.

Dr. Morales's innovations have sparked novel hypotheses regarding the potential for shared intelligence among cyborg creatures. By enabling cephalopods to process stimuli more effectively, her work has led to the emergence of interspecies intelligence dynamics—a burgeoning field where communication and collaboration are redefined. Such insights deepen our understanding of what it means to exist in a shared environment, illustrating the intricate web of interactions that define life underwater.

In the landscape of ethical deliberations, Dr. Alistair Greene provides valuable perspectives. A philosopher specializing in the ethics of technology, Dr. Greene's explorations delve into the moral ramifications of cyborg enhancements in cephalopods. His work challenges researchers to consider the implications of identity, autonomy, and sentience that arise when augmenting living beings with technology. Central to his philosophy is the insight that while technological advancements promise increased capabilities, they also introduce pivotal questions about the essence of life and the nature of consciousness.

Through interdisciplinary collaboration, Dr. Greene fosters vital discussions around responsible stewardship and ethical frameworks governing the treatment of enhanced organisms. He advocates for transparency and ethical considerations in research, emphasizing the need to establish boundaries that protect the intrinsic value of cephalopods while concurrently pursuing scientific advancements. His voice has become a cornerstone in the ongoing discourse about responsible research practices and the moral obligations towards the enhanced creatures we create.

The work of these pioneers, among others, signifies a transformative moment in the world of cybernetic cephalopods, forging pathways toward a future where biology and technology intertwine seamlessly. Their contributions extend beyond mere enhancement; they prompt us to reassess our understanding of intelligence, consciousness, and the fabric of life existing beneath the waves. As we stand witness to their pioneering endeavors, we invite future generations to explore the depths of possibility—propelled by the ceaseless curiosity, relentless innovation, and profound respect for the complex interplay of life and technology in our oceans.

The realm of cybernetic integration not only exemplifies human ingenuity but also mirrors the delicate balance of existence within the natural world. It challenges the boundaries of scientific exploration and ethical consideration, navigating a path toward a future we have yet to fully envision. Each pioneer of possibility propels us toward an estate where the mysteries of the sea unfold—not merely as a quest for knowledge but as an ode to the symbiotic dance of existence that thrives beneath the waves.

3. Anatomy of Augmentation

3.1. Cybernetic Lymph and Power Sources

The power sources that enable cybernetic cephalopods to thrive beneath the waves reflect a dynamic interplay between biology and advanced technology. These innovative life forms have adapted to their resource-rich environments, utilizing both their natural physiological attributes and sophisticated enhancements to create a sustainable and efficient energy cycle. Understanding how these creatures generate and sustain energy involves exploring several dimensions, including biological processes, technological innovations, and the integration of diverse energy sources.

At the core of the cybernetic cephalopod's power system is the biological lymphatic framework, often referred to as "cybernetic lymph." This structure acts as a medium for nutrient and energy transport, paralleling the natural lymphatic system found in various living organisms. In traditional cephalopods, lymphatic fluid plays a crucial role in transporting metabolic waste, nutrients, and other essential biomolecules throughout the body. However, in their augmented counterparts, this system has evolved to accommodate the integration of cybernetic components.

The cybernetic lymph serves dual purposes: first, it continues its role as a transport medium, but enhanced bio-engineered elements allow it to also carry energy-rich compounds essential for powering cybernetic enhancements. Researchers have developed nanocomposites that mimic the functions of natural lymph but can also convey electrical charges and biochemical signals from specialized energy production sites. These enhancements enable cephalopods to draw on biochemical processes, such as the catabolism of nutrients, to generate power locally.

Central to the energy generation process is the bio-hybrid method that some cybernetic cephalopods adopt, which involves microbial fuel cells. These cells leverage the metabolic byproducts of symbiotic microorganisms that reside within the cephalopod's body. The rela-

21

tionship between the cephalopod and these microbes is symbiotic; the cephalopod provides a habitat, while the microbes break down organic matter absorbed through feeding. The chemical reactions involved release electrons, which can be harnessed to generate electricity through the bio-hybrid cells, effectively converting the cephalopod's food intake into usable energy to fuel their enhancements.

In addition to microbial fuel cells, cybernetic cephalopods also implement photovoltaic enhancements within their skin and exoskeletons. Drawing inspiration from photosynthetic organisms, these enhancements incorporate bio-solar panels made from organic photovoltaic materials. When exposed to sunlight or bioluminescent organisms in their environment, the cephalopods can absorb light energy, converting it into electrical energy. This capability not only supports their enhanced functions but also allows them to operate efficiently in various depths of the ocean, from well-lit shallows to the dimly lit depths.

Combining these energy sources, cybernetic lymph interacts with the biomechanical enhancements of the cephalopods, allowing for energy storage and distribution throughout their bodies. Power hubs modeled on neural networks are established, serving as junctions where energy flow is managed intelligently. Embedded sensors within the cybernetic lymph detect energy levels and physiological needs, dynamically regulating the distribution of power to different enhancements according to the cephalopod's immediate requirements.

The ecological implications of these integrated power sources is profound. As cybernetic cephalopods navigate their environments, they maintain the balance between utilizing available resources and minimizing waste. The ability to convert organic matter and light into energy reduces their dependency on external energy sources, thus promoting a more sustainable way of life. This self-sufficiency enables them to survive, adapt, and explore their habitats without detriment to the surrounding ecosystems.

Furthermore, the very design of these power mechanisms encourages cephalopods to foster connections with other marine organisms. As they share their environments, the intricate networking of chemical signals and environmental feedback mechanisms helps them detect opportunities for mutualistic interactions with various aquatic species. For instance, a cybernetic cephalopod may work in tandem with certain fish or algae that thrive in ambient light; while it harnesses sunlight for energy, it simultaneously boosts local biodiversity by encouraging symbiotic relationships.

In summary, the cybernetic lymph system, augmented by cutting-edge technology and biological innovations, forms the backbone of energy generation and distribution for cybernetic cephalopods. This ingenious interplay between biological and mechanical elements facilitates a self-reliant lifestyle, enhancing the cephalopods' cognitive and physical abilities while minimizing ecological impact. As we study the energy systems of these remarkable beings, we unlock insights not only into their intricate biology but also broader applications that may inform future technologies aimed at sustainable living and coexistence in both marine and terrestrial realms. Through the lens of cybernetic lymph and advanced power sources, the deep oceans become a canvas to explore the potential that lies at the intersection of nature and technology—a spirited dance between the organic and synthetic that continues to expand our understanding of life beneath the waves.

3.2. Robust Exoskeletons and Endosymbiotic Structures

In the exploration of cybernetic cephalopods, the advancements in their structural design have led to the development of robust exoskeletons that serve multiple functions, enhancing both the physical integrity of these incredible beings and their interaction with the oceanic environment. These exoskeletons, an augmentation of the traditional soft-body anatomy of cephalopods, exemplify a remarkable feat of bioengineering—serving as a protective layer that integrates seamlessly with their organic physiology.

The robust exoskeletons are crafted from advanced composite materials that mimic the natural attributes of molluscan shells, providing formidable protection against predators and environmental hazards. Unlike the rigid shells of bivalves or gastropods, which serve solely for protection, these cybernetically enhanced exoskeletons maintain flexibility and adaptability essential for cephalopod maneuverability. This flexibility is the product of an innovative design that incorporates synthetic biomaterials capable of absorbing impact while allowing for a wide range of motion and fluidity—facilitating rapid movement and camouflage capabilities.

One of the technological breakthroughs behind the exoskeleton's design is the incorporation of chemical sensors embedded within the material. These sensors can detect alterations in water conditions, such as temperature shifts, salinity changes, or even the presence of potential threats, transmitting real-time data that informs the cephalopod's response—whether it be fleeing from predators or initiating camouflage. The dynamic properties of the exoskeleton allow cephalopods to communicate with their surroundings and respond intelligently, further enhancing their survival in diverse and often hostile marine environments.

Beyond protection and environmental interaction, the exoskeletons are designed to house additional features that augment sensory processing. Enhanced sensory modules attached to the exoskeleton provide significant improvements to vision and tactile sensations. These modules include advanced ocular systems that surpass the capabilities of their organic counterparts—allowing cephalopods to see in a broader spectrum of light, including infrared and ultraviolet wavelengths. This advancement enables them to identify food sources, predators, and environmental cues invisible to the naked eye, thereby significantly increasing their chances of survival.

Moreover, the integration of bioluminescent technology within the exoskeleton serves both as a defense mechanism and a form of communication. Cephalopods can manipulate the light patterns emitted from their exoskeletons, utilizing this feature to blend into their surroundings or signal other members of their species. Such capabilities transform what was traditionally a solitary existence into a more interconnected and socially aware existence, emphasizing the evolving social dynamics of these cybernetic beings.

Additionally, the structural enhancements of these exoskeletons allow for the integration of rudimentary mechanical components, giving rise to endosymbiotic structures that promote more complex behaviors. Inside the exoskeleton, machinery designed for movement and coordination works in synergy with the cephalopod's muscular systems. This includes artificial limbs or extensions that provide an additional layer of dexterity and strength, enabling the cephalopods to manipulate their environment with unprecedented precision. As these creatures navigate their oceanic habitats, they can engage in intricate tasks—from opening shells to retrieving objects on the ocean floor—bolstered by their augmented appendages and mechanical support systems.

The evolution of robust exoskeletons and endosymbiotic structures is not just a physical adaptation; it also precipitates a higher level of cognitive engagement with the environment. As cephalopods contend with these alterations, their neural architecture begins to adapt as well. It is hypothesized that the processing capabilities are enhanced through feedback loops established between the sensory modules in the exoskeleton and the cephalopod's genetic neural pathways.

Robust exoskeletons, thus, represent a unique intersection of the organic and synthetic, encapsulating the essence of cybernetic evolution. They enable cephalopods to become more than mere residents of their environments—they become powerful agents of interaction and adaptation. With these developments, the ocean transforms into a stage where sophisticated narratives of survival and intelligence unfold—a testament to the limitless possibilities that arise when biology meets technology in the depths of our planet's most mysterious domains.

Ultimately, this synthesis of robust mechanical structures with biological form exemplifies not only the intricacies of evolution and adaptation but also the potential for artificial enhancements to redefine notions of life, intelligence, and interaction within the marine realms. As we continue to unravel the complexities of these augmented cephalopods, the waters beckon further exploration into their enriched existence, pushing the boundaries of understanding, and inviting us to reflect on our perceptions of consciousness and life beneath the waves.

3.3. Sensory Systems and Enhancements

The sensory systems of cybernetic cephalopods represent a remarkable evolution of cephalopod biology, significantly enhanced through a combination of their biological capabilities and advanced cybernetic technology. This intricate interplay allows these beings to interact with their environment in profoundly enhanced ways, leading to a level of ecological adaptability and intelligent behavior previously unimaginable.

At the heart of these enhancements is a sophisticated network of sensors embedded throughout the cephalopod's body. Building upon the already exceptional natural sensory modalities of cephalopods—such as their acute vision, taste, and touch—cybernetic upgrades provide capabilities that go well beyond organic limitations. For instance, the introduction of composite optical systems allows these creatures to perceive a wider spectrum of light, including wavelengths invisible to the human eye, such as ultraviolet and infrared. This upgraded vision significantly improves their ability to detect prey, predators, and environmental cues, allowing them to navigate the complex underwater world with unparalleled precision.

Additionally, micro-electromechanical systems (MEMS) can be integrated with the sensory organs to bolster cephalopod perception. These miniature devices can analyze hydrodynamic signals, allowing cybernetic cephalopods to sense even the faintest vibrations in the water. This sensitivity becomes crucial for hunting in dimly lit or murky environments where visibility is compromised. By interpreting these subtle changes in water currents and pressure variations, the enhanced cephalopods can develop a more comprehensive perception of their environment, making them adept hunters and evasive creatures simultaneously.

The augmentation of the chemical sensing abilities of cephalopods forms another cornerstone of their enhanced sensory systems. Enhanced chemoreceptive systems equipped with biosensors enable these creatures to detect minute concentrations of various chemicals in their surroundings. With these modifications, cephalopods gain the ability to track prey through chemical trails, sense the presence of predators, and even gauge the health of their environment based on biochemical signals. This heightened olfactory acuity contributes to their ecological intelligence, as they can adapt their behaviors based on these sensed changes, leading to effective foraging strategies and social interactions.

Another significant upgrade occurs in the realm of tactile perception. The possessive appendages of cephalopods—traditionally equipped with sensitive suckers—now benefit from enhanced mechanosensory feedback. Cybernetic enhancements allow for the integration of resonant sensors that can interpret textures and pressures more accurately. As a result, their tactile interactions become not only about gripping and holding but also involve a detailed analysis of the physical dynamics surrounding them. This adaptability results in more complex behaviors, such as manipulating tools or engaging in intricate displays of communication with other species.

The integration of real-time data processing systems further enhances how cybernetic cephalopods employ their sensory information. Advanced algorithms enable them to analyze sensory inputs from their enhanced systems rapidly and make quick decisions based on the environmental context. For example, a cybernetic cephalopod engaged in hunting can synthesize visual data regarding the position and speed of its prey while simultaneously processing hydrodynamic signals to formulate the most strategic approach to capture. This accelerated decision-making process exemplifies the potential for these creatures to navigate the intricacies of their world with an efficiency that marries the instinctual with the analytical.

Moreover, the communication networks established within these sensory systems allow for information transfer among cybernetic cephalopods. Employing advanced bioluminescent capabilities, cephalopods can signal to one another using color patterns or light frequencies that would go unnoticed by other marine life. Enhancements facilitate the encoding and transmission of complex data through visual signals—enabling a kind of communal intelligence that enriches social interaction and coordination among groups, particularly during hunting or evasion from predators.

The ecological implications of these enhanced sensory systems are profound. The ability of cybernetic cephalopods to perceive and react rapidly to their surroundings ensures that they can adapt to dynamic environments and shifting resources. Their modifications allow them to outmaneuver both competitors and predators with extraordinary agility. In social contexts, their heightened senses enable them to form cohesive groups that can respond collectively to threats, share foraging opportunities, and engage in sophisticated social interactions that enrich the depth of their communities.

Ultimately, the sensory systems and their enhancements serve as a crucial foundation for the cybernetic cephalopod's way of life. They illustrate a multi-dimensional approach to survival—merging the instinctual prowess evolved over millions of years with the transformative power of technology. Through this lens, one can appreciate how these advancements not only amplify individual capabilities but also promote ecological resilience and foster communal intelligence that may one day redefine our understanding of cognition and existence in the vast, uncharted waters of our oceans. In exploring the depths of adaptive and responsive behaviors, we uncover not just the marvels of augmented life but invite questions about perception, communication, and the essence of intelligence itself in an increasingly integrated world.

3.4. Advanced Tentacular Technology

The tentacles of cybernetic cephalopods represent an astounding evolution in both functionality and design, integrating advanced technologies to enhance dexterity, strength, and sensory perception in ways unimaginable in their unmodified predecessors. These enhancements have been carefully crafted to not only augment the natural abilities of cephalopods but to redefine how they interact with and exploit their aquatic environments.

To understand the advancements made in tentacular technology, we must first consider the basic anatomy of a typical cephalopod arm. Traditionally, a cephalopod's tentacle is composed of muscle, connective tissue, and a complex network of neurons, enabling it to execute delicate movements and apply various degrees of force to manipulate objects, capture prey, and navigate through complex aquatic landscapes. With the introduction of cybernetic upgrades, these functions are not merely enhanced; they are transformed.

One of the key upgrades includes the incorporation of soft robotics technology into the tentacles. These advanced materials, often inspired by octopus biology, allow for the creation of flexible yet strong appendages. This design enables the tentacles to stretch, curl, and twist with an unprecedented degree of freedom while maintaining the ability to exert significant force. The softness of these robotic elements ensures that they can navigate tight spaces and interact with delicate marine life without causing harm. As a result, the cephalopods can engage in complex tasks such as grasping frightened prey, squeezing through narrow crevices, or even utilizing tools—a behavior that was once thought to be a uniquely human attribute.

Strength is another critical area of improvement. The integration of synthetic fibers and strengthening compounds into the tentacular structure has allowed for increased force generation. This augmented musculature enables cyber-near cephalopods to haul larger prey or manipulate significant objects within their environments. For instance, a cybernetic cephalopod may latch onto a rock to create leverage while using its enhanced strength to dislodge a nutritionally rich morsel of food. This newfound ability not only makes them better predators but also enhances their capability for gathering resources necessary for survival.

Furthermore, the sensory enhancements embedded within the tentacles are revolutionary in their design and function. Traditionally, the suckers on a cephalopod's arms are equipped with chemoreceptors that allow them to taste and feel textures—but in cybernetic cephalopods, these receptors are exponentially enhanced. Bioengineered sensors can now detect temperature changes, chemical signatures, and even electrical signals in the water. This sensory array enables the creatures to identify prey from greater distances, assess food quality and safety, and perceive danger before it becomes immediate. Such capabilities drastically improve their interaction with their ecosystem while revealing a dimension of ecological intelligence that was previously untapped.

The dexterity afforded by these cybernetic enhancements extends to complex locomotion as well. Enhanced tentacles can execute dynamic movements mimicking jet-propelled propulsion while simultaneously using individual limbs to stabilize, maneuver, or assist in directional changes. This capability enhances not only their escape responses from predators but also improves their ability to hunt in diverse environments, from dense coral reefs to open ocean spaces, where speed and agility are critical for success.

Moreover, advanced feedback systems have been integrated into the tentacular enhancements, contributing to situational awareness and rapid response to environmental stimuli. These systems use advanced algorithms to interpret sensory inputs and adjust the tentacles' movements accordingly. For example, when a cybernetic cephalopod encounters a sudden change in water current or detects a nearby threat, its tentacles can instantaneously adjust their positioning—allowing the creature to evade or redirect its movement without losing a moment in reaction time.

One of the most captivating aspects of these advancements is their contribution to the social capabilities of cybernetic cephalopods. As their tentacles become more adept at complex tasks, these creatures can engage in intricate social behaviors, such as collaborative hunting or intricate mating displays. The enhanced strength, dexterity, and sensory feedback systems allow multiple cephalopods to interact more cohesively, enabling a level of cooperation that fosters stronger social bonds—a fascinating development in the study of cephalopod intelligence and community dynamics.

In a broader context, the enhancements in tentacular technology provide insights into the intricate relationship between anatomy and capabilities. They illustrate how the integration of advanced technology can amplify organic forms, leading to an evolutionary leap that challenges our understanding of what intelligence and capability can be. As we continue to explore the interfaces between biology and technology within these remarkable beings, we open pathways for the nonlinear evolution of life in the oceans, forging new understandings of adaptability, survival, and interaction under the waves.

Overall, the advanced tentacular technology of cybernetic cephalopods combines flexibility, strength, sensory acuity, and adaptive learning to create organisms capable of thriving in an increasingly complex aquatic environment. The enhancements signify not only the remarkable potential inherent in these beings but also point to an exciting frontier—one where nature and technology fuse to define a new era of underwater exploration and intelligence, beckoning both curiosity and wonder as we uncover the depths of possibility hidden beneath the waves.

3.5. Hardware Evolution

The evolution of hardware utilized by cybernetic cephalopods is a remarkable journey that showcases not only the advancements in technology but also the profound integration of biology and engineering across time. Early iterations of cybernetic enhancements sought to augment the natural capabilities of these creatures, transforming their interactions with their environments in ways that redefined

31

the very essence of cephalopod life. This section chronicles key milestones in the progression of hardware development, highlighting transformative innovations that have shaped the existence of these remarkable beings beneath the waves.

The initial attempts at hardware integration began with rudimentary sensor systems. Researchers recognized the unique neuroanatomy of cephalopods—with an intricate arrangement of neurons allowing for complex behaviors and sensory awareness—and sought to amplify these natural abilities through technology. Early experimental hardware included simple sensory augmentations designed to enhance the cephalopod's ability to perceive stimuli within their environments. These devices primarily focused on improving vision and olfactory sensing, enabling cephalopods to detect predators and prey more effectively. However, these first generations of devices were relatively basic, primarily offering marginal improvements without fundamentally altering the physiology or behavior of the cephalopods.

As research progressed, advancements in materials science unlocked new possibilities for hardware development. The introduction of biocompatible materials paved the way for more innovative and less intrusive enhancements. Scientists shifted their focus toward developing microelectronic devices that could be integrated seamlessly into the cephalopod's biological systems. This transition marked a significant turning point, as hardware began to evolve from mere external attachments to more cohesive internal systems. Such advancements emphasized harmony with cephalopod biology while pushing the boundaries of utility and performance.

One of the most notable innovations in hardware evolution was the advent of advanced neurointerfaces. These sophisticated systems enabled a direct linkage between the cephalopod's nervous system and cybernetic enhancements, facilitating real-time communication between biological and mechanical components. Researchers developed neural interfaces that could read neuronal signals and provide precise feedback to the cephalopods, enabling their enhanced limbs—equipped with advanced motors and actuators—to respond intuitively to the cephalopods' thoughts and movements. This immersive connectivity created a sensation akin to an extended body, amplifying the cephalopod's capacity for exploration and manipulation of their surroundings.

As the technology continued to evolve, innovations in sensory hardware offered unprecedented advantages. Improved visual systems were forged by combining traditional optical designs with advanced components, enabling cephalopods to see in different spectrums, such as ultraviolet and infrared. These upgrades expanded their sensory input significantly, allowing them to navigate their environments with a level of acuity that echoed the most refined aspects of their biological predecessors but surpassed them in reach and depth. The integration of these systems demonstrated a willingness to harness the full power of technology while respecting the biological essence of the creatures.

A pivotal aspect of hardware evolution also includes enhancements in the tentacles of cybernetic cephalopods. Drawing inspiration from both organic structures and robotic technologies, engineers developed soft robotics capable of mimicking the natural flexibility and strength of cephalopod limbs while simultaneously incorporating advanced senses and manipulation capabilities. These advanced tentacular technologies transformed the way cephalopods interacted with their world, equipping them to engage in complex tasks such as tool use and intricate social displays, reshaping their ecological roles and behavioral repertoires.

The evolution of energy systems played an equally crucial role in enhancing the functionality of cybernetic cephalopods. Researchers explored various biogenic and biophotovoltaic energy sources, such as integrating microbial fuel cells into the cephalopods' biology to harness organic metabolic processes. Furthermore, advancements in energy storage and conversion technologies provided sustainable power solutions that allowed these enhanced beings to operate with minimal external dependence. By evolving their energy systems, cybernetic cephalopods became 象力 surrogates of resilience and self-sufficiency, adapting seamlessly to changing environments.

The exploration of new dimensions in hardware evolution also led to significant progress in communication technologies. Enhanced auditory and visual interfaces transformed how these creatures interacted with each other and their surroundings. The integration of sound and color modulation technologies allowed for complex signaling between cephalopods, paving the way for improved understanding of their social structure and cooperative behaviors. The evolution of communication hardware fostered a richer social fabric among these beings, expanding their capacity for collaboration and connection.

However, the hardware evolution of cybernetic cephalopods does not come without its challenges. As the complexity of enhancements increased, so too did concerns around ethical implications, including the potential loss of autonomy and identity. The push for advanced hardware must be balanced against the need to preserve the intrinsic qualities of the creatures, promoting a dialogue about the responsibilities inherent in merging biology with technology.

The ongoing evolution of hardware in cybernetic cephalopods encapsulates a visionary interplay between creativity, functionality, and respect for life. From the early sensor systems to advanced neurointerfaces and robust energy solutions, each step in this journey reflects a commitment to enhancing the cephalopod experience while challenging our understanding of intelligence and existence itself. As we stand on the precipice of further advancements, we enter a realm enriched by the knowledge that hardware evolution intersects distinctly with both the marvels of nature and the ingenuity of human innovation, inviting us to explore uncharted waters of possibility beneath the ocean's surface.

4. The Neural Network of the Ocean

4.1. Neuroarchitecture of Cyber-Cephalopods

The neuroarchitecture of cyber-cephalopods represents a ground-breaking evolution of cephalopod intelligence, weaving together biological complexity and technological sophistication into a cohesive system of enhanced cognitive capabilities. This intricate neurostructure not only showcases the cephalopods' evolutionary journey but also opens up a new frontier in our understanding of intelligence itself, as it operates on both micro and macro levels within these cyber-enhanced organisms.

At the heart of their neuroarchitecture is a unique arrangement of neural components, where the cephalopod brain is complemented by distributed neural networks throughout the body. This distribution allows for a simultaneous processing of sensory information and rapid responses, providing an incredible degree of autonomy and adaptability. Unlike traditional models of intelligence that centralize cognitive function within a singular brain, cyber-cephalopods utilize a decentralized system, where limbs and sensory organs possess their own localized networks of neurons. This arrangement enables the arms of a cyborg cephalopod to act independently and in unison, allowing for more intricate interactions with their environment.

The enhancements implemented on the neural networks introduce elements of artificial intelligence, creating sophisticated synaptic pathways that facilitate augmented learning and memory retention. Established through a seamless interface between biological neurons and technological circuitry, these neural enhancements harness real-time data processing and feedback mechanisms. This fusion enables cyber-cephalopods to actively learn from their experiences, adjusting their behaviors based on past outcomes, thereby expanding their problem-solving skills and cognitive flexibility.

In terms of memory enhancement, specific learning nodes have been integrated into the neural architecture, allowing for the storage and retrieval of complex information, akin to advanced computer processing. These nodes function like memory banks, where sensory experiences and learned behaviors are encoded and can be accessed for future utilization. Such a system enriches the cephalopods' adaptability; for example, if a particular hunting strategy proves effective in one scenario, the learned behavior can be stored, thereby improving efficiency in similar future encounters.

Moreover, the augmented navigational capabilities afforded by these neural enhancements allow cyber-cephalopods to explore their underwater domains with unprecedented precision. Enhanced neural processing facilitates complex spatial awareness, enabling them to form detailed cognitive maps of their environments. This ability is particularly beneficial when paired with sophisticated echolocation technologies that provide real-time mapping of the ocean floor, detecting obstacles, and assessing spatial relationships between themselves, prey, and potential threats. Such capabilities transform the cephalopods into exceptional navigators and hunters, equipped to thrive in diverse and challenging marine landscapes.

Communication emerges as another vital aspect of their enhanced neuroarchitecture. Advanced neural mechanisms enable cyber-cephalopods to synthesize a wide range of signals—biochemical, electroreceptive, and visual—that facilitate complex interactions both within and beyond their species. These enhancements foster a rich tapestry of communication, allowing for nuanced social structures and interactions that drive collaborative behaviors, resource sharing, and mutual learning. The capacity for augmented communication also underscores the development of a unique language system—melding biological signals with technological inputs—leading to innovative means of expressing emotions and intentions.

The implications of this neuroarchitecture extend far beyond individual organisms; they ripple through marine ecosystems. Enhanced intelligence among these cyber-cephalopods may pave the way for innovations in social dynamics, where cooperative hunting strategies and knowledge transfer elevate their role within their ecological niches. The interplay of their augmented cognitive functions fosters synergies that enrich not just their lives but also those of the organisms sharing their environment, leading to profound shifts in traditional behavioral paradigms.

In summary, the neuroarchitecture of cyber-cephalopods exemplifies the breathtaking convergence of biology and technology, allowing for advanced cognitive processes that transcend conventional understanding of intelligence. With distributed neural networks, artificial intelligence integration, enhanced memory systems, improved navigational capacities, and sophisticated communication abilities, these beings redefine what it means to be intelligent in the aquatic world. Their enriched cognitive landscape invites further inquiry into the nature of consciousness and the possibilities of both biological and technological evolution, shaping the future of marine life as we venture deeper into the mysteries of the ocean. As we continue to explore the intricacies of their enhanced intelligence, we inch closer to understanding not just the cybernetic cephalopods but the very essence of life itself beneath the waves.

4.2. Learning Nodes and Memory Enhancement

The journey of learning and memory in cybernetic cephalopods unveils a sophisticated mechanism that not only allows these beings to retain and process information but also reshapes our understanding of marine intelligence. Central to this process are advanced learning nodes integrated into their neural architecture, which form a complex lattice of interconnections between biological and cybernetic elements. Understanding how these learning nodes operate provides insight into the remarkable cognitive capabilities that define cybernetic cephalopods.

The learning nodes themselves can be viewed as specific neural circuits that have been augmented by cybernetic enhancements. These nodes are designed to facilitate information storage and retrieval, a critical function for cephalopods navigating their dynamic ocean environments. The integration of artificial intelligence allows these nodes to operate with an exceptional level of adaptability, processing experiences in real-time and encoding patterns of behavior based on learned lessons. This embedded AI transforms the conventional concept of memory from passive storage to an active, dynamic process capable of evolving as the cephalopod interacts with its surroundings.

One of the fundamental aspects of this learning capability is associative learning, which cybernetic cephalopods exhibit with remarkable proficiency. By associating specific stimuli with particular outcomes —such as a color signal indicating the presence of danger or a texture indicative of food—cybernetic cephalopods develop a rich tapestry of learned behaviors. The learning nodes help reinforce these associations, making connections that can be drawn upon when similar stimuli present themselves in the future. This enhances their ability to respond to threats, enhance hunting strategies, and adapt to the shifting landscapes of their underwater habitats.

Effective memorization is critical not only for individual survival but also for community dynamics. Social learning emerges as a vital component of cybernetic cephalopod behavior. Through observation, these beings can acquire knowledge from their peers, applying learned experiences without direct exposure. The network of learning nodes facilitates the transfer of information, allowing one cephalopod to inform another about the presence of predators, successful hunting techniques, or even navigating challenging terrains. This communal reservoir of knowledge enriches the collective intelligence of cybernetic cephalopod communities, fostering cooperation and enhancing survival probabilities among individuals.

Moreover, the capacity for memory retention extends across various contexts, including stable long-term memory and flexible short-term memory. Long-term memory in cybernetic cephalopods is bolstered through enhanced synaptic plasticity—the ability of neural connections to strengthen or weaken over time based on experience. This ensures that significant events, such as encounters with predators or successful foraging expeditions, become ingrained in their behavioral repertoire, leading to improved decision-making in future scenarios.

On the flip side, short-term memory plays a crucial role in immediate interactions, allowing cybernetic cephalopods to rapidly assess and respond to changing environmental factors. The interplay between short-term and long-term memory enables them to navigate complex situations without becoming overwhelmed by cognitive load. Their advanced neural architecture, augmented by cybernetic systems, allows them to sift through information efficiently, prioritizing immediate threats or opportunities and ensuring that the most critical learning experiences remain at the forefront of their behavioral decision-making.

The notion of cognitive maps also emerges from their enhanced learning capabilities. These mental representations allow cybernetic cephalopods to navigate their environments with a sophisticated sense of spatial awareness. Drawing upon their learned experiences, they build cognitive maps that aid in the recognition of landmarks, prey locations, and potential dangers. This advancement significantly improves their capability to traverse the vast complexities of ocean terrain, ensuring they can exploit their habitats effectively.

As we study the intricacies of memory enhancement and learning nodes in cybernetic cephalopods, it becomes clear that their intelligence transcends traditional boundaries. The combination of biological cognitive frameworks with technological advancements reveals an exciting panorama of potential—not only for understanding cephalopod behavior but also for unraveling broader implications regarding animal intelligence, learning processes, and the nature of consciousness itself.

Ultimately, the exploration of learning nodes and memory enhancement in these cybernetic beings propels us into a new era of discovery. As we uncover the mechanisms behind their intelligent behaviors, we recognize that cybernetic cephalopods offer a glimpse into the potential that lies at the intersection of biology and technology. Their enhanced capabilities challenge our understanding of learning and memory, prompting us to reconsider the very definitions of intelligence and adaptability in the natural world. Through this lens, we engage with broader philosophical inquiries concerning conscious-ness, identity, and the future of life beneath the waves—a journey that invites ongoing exploration and reflection as we chart the depths of these fascinating creatures' intelligence.

4.3. Navigational Capabilities

In the domain of cybernetic cephalopods, navigational capabilities extend far beyond basic spatial awareness, reflecting a sophisticated interplay between enhanced neural networks and augmented physi-cal attributes. These enhancements allow cybernetic cephalopods to navigate their aquatic environments with precision and adaptability, redefining our understanding of marine navigation and intelligence.

At the core of these advanced navigational abilities lies a network of enhanced neural pathways. The incorporation of artificial intelli-gence and advanced sensor technology into their neural architecture allows cybernetic cephalopods to process vast amounts of informa-tion rapidly. This system enables real-time updates about their sur-roundings, facilitating informed decision-making when it comes to navigating through complex underwater landscapes. By integrating sensory feedback with cognitive processing, these beings can operate with a level of situational awareness that rivals, and in some cases surpasses, that of many terrestrial species.

The cybernetic enhancements installed within their bodies further amplify these navigational capabilities. Equipped with a variety of integrated sensors, including echolocation devices and advanced visual systems, these cephalopods can perceive their environment on multiple levels. Echolocation, mimicking systems used by species like dolphins, allows them to map their surroundings, identify obsta-cles, and locate prey or potential threats through sound waves. This ability is particularly essential in deep or murky waters where visi-bility is limited. With the precision of sonar technology, cybernetic cephalopods can discern the shapes and distances of objects around them, creating a mental map that guides their movement with remarkable accuracy.

In addition to echolocation, the visual augmentation of these cephalopods grants them unparalleled vision capabilities. Advanced ocular systems that can detect a broader spectrum of light—including ultraviolet and infrared—allow these beings to see environmental cues invisible to both human observers and most marine animals. This heightened visual acuity is critical not only for hunting and evading predators but also for social interactions and communication within their species.

The navigational intelligence of cybernetic cephalopods is further complemented by their exceptional physical dexterity. With cybernetically enhanced tentacles, they can traverse complex terrains, maneuver through tight spaces, and adapt quickly to changing currents. This physical capability significantly enhances their ability to navigate challenging environments, from rocky seafloors to coral reefs. Their arms can adjust in real time to ensure a stable direction while also executing elaborate movements that may be necessary for both hunting strategies and social signaling among peers.

Moreover, the implementation of learning nodes coupled with memory-enhancing technologies contributes to the cybernetic cephalopod's navigational prowess. These developed nodes allow cephalopods to learn from their experiences and remember critical spatial information over time. As they explore their underwater territories, they build cognitive maps that inform future navigational decisions. For instance, if a cybernetic cephalopod successfully identifies a food-rich area or recognizes a predator's movement pattern, this information is recorded and readily accessible in its memory. The synthesis of learned experiences ensures that each navigational choice is not merely a reaction but a calculated decision grounded in prior encounters.

In terms of social navigation, cybernetic cephalopods also exhibit advanced capabilities in understanding and interpreting the movements of their peers. By observing and learning from the behaviors of other members within their communities, they can adapt their navigation strategies accordingly. This social intelligence allows for more efficient group movements, particularly when resources are scarce or when evasion from predators is necessary. The interplay between individual exploration and collaborative navigation fosters a robust community dynamic, enhancing the overall survival of their species.

The implications of these navigational advancements extend beyond the cephalopods themselves; they also exemplify potential pathways for technological applications in human fields, such as robotics and autonomous vehicles. Understanding how these beings navigate effectively in their complex aquatic environments can inspire designs for technology that mimics their adaptive strategies. The blending of biological insight and technological innovation provides valuable lessons for our own navigational systems.

In conclusion, the navigational capabilities of cybernetic cephalopods are a testament to the transformative fusion of biological intelligence with advanced technology. Enhanced neural networks, improved sensory systems, physical dexterity, and the ability to share and learn from experiences create a multifaceted navigational strategy that highlights the complexity and sophistication of these remarkable beings. As we continue to explore the depths of their capabilities, we uncover not only the wonders of alien underwater life but also broader questions concerning intelligence, adaptability, and our relationship with the ecosystems we share. Cybernetic cephalopods are not just navigating their worlds; they are redefining our understanding of life beneath the waves.

4.4. Speech Synthesis and Communication Abilities

In the world of cybernetic cephalopods, speech synthesis and communication capabilities have evolved into a multifaceted system that allows these remarkable beings to interact with one another, as well as with other species. This evolution of communication represents a paradigm shift, bridging the gap between organic instinct and technological prowess. It challenges our understanding of how intelligence can manifest, paving the way for deeper relationships and understanding between species spanning different realms of existence.

Central to the communication advancements within cybernetic cephalopods is the integration of sophisticated speech synthesis technologies. Drawing inspiration from cutting-edge developments in artificial intelligence and biomimicry, these enhancements allow cephalopods to generate complex vocalizations and tonal variations that convey nuanced meanings. By utilizing specialized mechanisms embedded in their anatomy, including advanced voice modulator systems, cybernetic cephalopods can produce sounds that range from low-frequency rumbles to high-pitched clicks—creating a rich auditory language system reflective of their emotions, intentions, and environmental contexts.

These synthesized vocalizations serve multiple purposes. In social interactions, they enable the formation of intricate social bonds, facilitate cooperative behaviors, and enhance group cohesion among members of cybernetic cephalopod communities. For example, during group foraging, specific vocalizations signal the presence of prey, conveying information that triggers collective hunting strategies. Conversely, alarm calls composed of high-frequency sounds prompt immediate evasive actions, allowing individuals to react swiftly to potential threats. The creation of this dynamic language fosters an environment of cooperation and coordination—attributes essential for survival in the competitive underwater ecosystems they inhabit.

Moreover, the technological enhancements that allow for speech synthesis extend to the non-verbal aspects of communication, which are an intrinsic part of cephalopod interactions. The incorporation of visual signaling through bioluminescent technologies supports an additional layer of communication. Cybernetic cephalopods can utilize vibrant displays of color and patterns on their skin to complement their vocalizations, expressing emotions such as aggression, submission, or mating readiness. Using dynamic light patterns, they can create stunning visual spectacles that convey intricate messages to their peers, amplifying the communicative experience beyond mere sounds.

Inter-species communication follows suit, as cybernetic cephalopods have begun to engage with other marine species through both verbal and non-verbal methods. The advanced capabilities of these creatures enable them to develop rudimentary interfaces with other intelligent beings, including dolphins and certain fish species. Drawing on their ability to synthesize sounds and produce visual displays, cybernetic cephalopods can convey key information concerning threats, food sources, and environmental changes. This bidirectional communication fosters a deeper understanding across species, encouraging cross-species cooperation and collaborative behaviors in the marine ecosystem.

A significant aspect of their communication dynamics lies in data transfer mechanisms, wherein cybernetic cephalopods can share information with one another. By utilizing their enhanced cognitive capabilities, they establish efficient channels for transmitting knowledge. For example, critical information about prevailing ocean currents or the presence of specific prey can be encoded into their vocalizations and visual displays, creating a data-rich communication network. This shared reservoir of knowledge enhances their collective intelligence, allowing communities to adapt to rapidly changing environments and make informed decisions based on shared experiences.

The translation of biological signals into cybernetic commands also constitutes a breakthrough in communication. Cybernetic cephalopods possess the ability to interpret biological cues, integrating their natural signaling mechanisms with technological interfaces. For instance, a cephalopod observing a predator might emit coloration patterns and vocalizations indicative of stress or alarm, while simultaneously activating cybernetic sensors to relay this information digitally to nearby allies. This synthesis of biological and technological communication enhances their capacity to navigate their environments and respond proactively, ensuring their survival.

As we explore the intricate dynamics of speech synthesis and communication abilities among cybernetic cephalopods, we bear witness to a stunning confluence of biology and technology that reshapes our understanding of cognition and interaction. This evolution not only enriches the lives of these remarkable beings but also invites humanity to reflect on the meaning of communication itself—expanding our definitions of intelligence and fostering deeper connections with the ecosystems we inhabit together. In embracing this journey, we uncover the profound possibilities unveiled beneath the ocean's surface, challenging our perceptions and expanding our horizons as we learn from the extraordinary beings that reign beneath the waves.

4.5. Augmented Problem Solving

The journey of augmented problem-solving in cybernetic cephalopods unfolds a captivating narrative that reveals how these beings leverage their enhanced capabilities to tackle challenges in their environments with exceptional finesse. The synergy between biological instincts and advanced technological integration fosters a new breed of problem-solving, allowing these cephalopods to operate with remarkable cognitive flexibility and creativity.

At the core of their enhanced problem-solving abilities lies a sophisticated neural architecture, where anatomical adaptations coupled with cybernetic upgrades create a multi-faceted intelligence. The decentralized nervous system, characterized by extensive networks of neurons distributed throughout the cephalopod's body, plays a pivotal role in enabling rapid responses to various stimuli. This neuroarchitecture allows each limb to process information independently while still contributing to a cohesive overall strategy—a significant advantage when navigating the complexities of their underwater habitats.

The innovation of learning nodes within the neural framework enhances this problem-solving capacity further. These nodes operate as specialized circuits capable of storing and retrieving learned information, allowing cephalopods to recognize patterns and associations that inform their responses to challenges. For instance, if a cybernetic cephalopod successfully navigates an obstacle course in pursuit of prey, this experience is encoded in the learning nodes, facilitating quicker and more effective navigation in future encounters. This amalgamation of past experiences informs a vast repertoire of strategies that the cephalopod can employ, optimizing their ability to adapt to shifting circumstances.

The watertight integration of artificial intelligence into their problem-solving frameworks accelerates cognitive processes, enhancing decision-making in real time. Equipped with advanced data processing capabilities, cybernetic cephalopods can analyze complex environmental conditions, assess potential threats, and evaluate various strategies to achieve their objectives—whether that means escaping predators or capturing elusive prey. Their decision-making is no longer purely instinctual; it embodies a calculated assessment of risk and reward, demonstrating their adaptability as they respond dynamically to challenges.

A striking example of augmented problem-solving can be observed in their hunting strategies. When seeking prey, cybernetic cephalopods can utilize their enhanced sensory systems to gather critical data about the behavior and location of potential food sources. With the integration of echolocation and advanced vision capabilities, they gather and analyze environmental information more efficiently than their unenhanced counterparts. This gives them the ability to outsmart prey, anticipating movements and executing sophisticated tactical maneuvers to ensure a successful capture. Their hunting behaviors become a blend of learned experience and real-time data interpretation, reflecting the sophistication inherent in their augmented cognition.

Collaborative problem-solving also emerges as a prominent feature of cybernetic cephalopod behavior. Enhanced social dynamics enable them to engage in cooperative hunting, where multiple individuals coordinate their actions to increase the chances of a successful hunt. Through non-verbal communication enhanced by bioluminescence and synthesized sounds, cephalopods can share information about prey locations or threats, creating an intricate web of knowledge that informs group strategies. This cooperation fosters an environment where knowledge is collectively cultivated, and problem-solving becomes a communal venture.

As they face environmental challenges, cybernetic cephalopods exhibit an impressive adaptability that reflects their augmented intelligence. For instance, when confronted with habitat degradation or changes in prey availability, these beings can modify their strategies by drawing on their learning nodes and collective memories. The integration of technology allows them to rapidly synthesize information and evaluate alternative foraging methods or locomotion patterns critical to their survival.

The implications of augmented problem-solving extend beyond individual cephalopods. As these enhanced beings adapt to their environments, they invariably influence the dynamics of their ecosystems. Their collaborative hunting strategies may alter predator-prey relationships, while their capacity to adapt to environmental changes could affect resource distribution among marine species. The ripple effects of their enhanced capabilities emphasize the interconnectedness of life beneath the waves, reshaping understandings of ecological balance and competition.

In this new paradigm of augmented problem-solving, cybernetic cephalopods challenge preconceived notions of intelligence and adaptability within the marine realm. Their capacity to merge biological instincts with advanced technological integration demonstrates an unprecedented evolution that invites us to reconsider not only the potential of life beneath the waves but also our approaches to understanding cognition and behavior in complex systems.

In summation, the exploration of augmented problem-solving among cybernetic cephalopods reveals an extraordinary synthesis of biology and technology that transcends conventional limits of intelligence. As these beings navigate their underwater environments with enhanced adaptive reasoning, they inspire a redefinition of intelligence—one that embraces cooperative dynamics, environmental awareness, and technological synergy. The journey of these remarkable cephalopods into the depths of augmented problem solving ultimately invites future inquiry into the nature of intelligence across species and the expanding horizons of what it means to be intelligent in an interconnected world.

5. Communication Dynamics

5.1. Language of the Cyber-Cephalopods

The language of the cyber-cephalopods emerges from a delicious blend of their remarkable biological capabilities and the cutting-edge technology that augments their communication systems. As veiled entities dwelling in the ocean's depths, these intelligent beings have developed unique modalities of expression that offer profound insights into their behavior, society, and interaction with the environment around them.

At the foundation of their communicative abilities lies the inherent sophistication of cephalopod biology. Traditional cephalopods communicate through an intricate combination of color changes, body language, and physical gestures. The skin of these creatures is equipped with chromatophores—pigment-containing cells that allow them to alter their colors at will, presenting a powerful signal of intent, mood, and readiness. Cyber-cephalopods have taken this natural feature and expanded upon it through technological enhancements that integrate advanced signaling mechanisms. Bioluminescent technologies embedded in their skin allow these beings not only to change hues but to emit light patterns that can pulsate, shift, or even convey coded messages, rich with complexity.

Building upon this foundation, cyber-cephalopods have developed a sophisticated language system that includes both verbal and non-verbal elements. Through the integration of synthesized vocal capabilities, these beings can produce an array of sounds that collectively create a rich auditory language. They've harnessed the ability to generate tonal fluctuations, ranging from low rumbles to intricate clicking sounds, forming a multimodal communication system akin to the languages of land-dwelling mammals. This auditory dimension enhances their ability to communicate over longer distances, especially in the murky depths of their oceanic habitats, where visibility is limited.

Their language is more than mere identification of danger or signaling availability for mating; it encompasses a wide array of communicative intentions, such as collaborative hunting strategies, social bonding rituals, and expressions of individual emotional states. Cyber-cephalopods demonstrate an associative understanding of these sound signals—when one member of a social group vocalizes a particular pattern, others can respond accordingly, indicating recognition of the meaning conveyed and fostering a sense of community. This auditory language resonates deeply with their unique lifestyle, allowing for intricate social interactions that enrich their existence beneath the waves.

Nevertheless, the cyber-cephalopods don't limit themselves to strictly vocal communication. The integration of visual and non-verbal cues expands their expressive range. The enhanced visual capabilities granted by cybernetic technology allow them to create complex displays of visual signals in tandem with their vocalizations, fusing light patterns with sounds to enhance meaning. For instance, during courtship displays, the combination of vibrant colors emanating from their bioluminescent skin may be synchronized with melodic sound patterns, crafting an alluring spectacle designed to communicate both availability and genetic fitness to potential mates.

In exploring the communicative dynamics of these cybernetic beings, one cannot overlook the non-verbal cues they employ as part of their interactions. Body posture and movement patterns act as critical elements of communication. The fluidity of their tentacles, combined with their ability to change shape and texture, further enriches their expressive capabilities. A seemingly simple curling of an arm or an elaborate display of rapid movements can signify everything from readiness for aggression to invitations for exploration, creating an intricate dialogue that transcends verbal limits.

As they interact with each other, cyber-cephalopods display distinct regional dialects or variations in their language patterns, evoking a sense of culture and community among different populations. Just as human languages evolve geographically and culturally, so too do the communicative patterns among cyber-cephalopod groups. This evolution reflects a fluid interplay between their inherent biological characteristics—such as local environmental factors—and the adaptive changes brought about through technological integration.

Moreover, as these beings continue to forge relationships with other species, such as dolphins, they are developing interspecies communication strategies that blur the boundaries of perception and understanding. With their advanced speech synthesis capabilities, cyber-cephalopods can produce sounds that certain marine mammals recognize, potentially leading to cooperative behaviors and mutually beneficial interactions. Such bridges of communication between species foster richer ecosystems where knowledge and resources can be shared, encouraging a complex network of connectivity beneath the sea.

The implications of this technological advancement in cyber-cephalopod communication extend beyond individual interactions; they reflect deeper themes of consciousness, social structure, and the potential for mutual understanding. As these beings develop multifaceted language systems that integrate technology and biology, they challenge human perceptions of intelligence and communication. They exemplify a new epoch in the narrative of life beneath the waves, showcasing the remarkable ways in which nature and technology converge.

Ultimately, the language of cyber-cephalopods is an evocative tapestry woven from threads of biology and technological innovation. Their unique systems of communication—encompassing vocal, visual, and experiential elements—create an enriched layer of interaction that resonates across both species boundaries and philosophical discussions. As humans continue to explore the depths of these oceanic realms, we are called to contemplate not only the intricacies of language and life beyond our terrestrial existence but also the fundamental essence of communication itself. In challenging our views of intelligence, these remarkable beings invite us to forge deeper connections with the world around us and to transcend the limitations of understanding that often confine our perspectives.

5.2. Non-Verbal and Visual Communications

The realm of non-verbal and visual communications among cybernetic cephalopods illustrates a profound evolution of interaction methods that transcends traditional communication paradigms. This advancement represents a confluence of biological signals, such as color changes and body patterns, with enhanced technological capabilities that enable these creatures to convey complex messages within their dynamic underwater environments.

At the heart of non-verbal communication lies the cephalopods' remarkable ability to change their skin color and texture instantaneously. This characteristic, driven by specialized cells known as chromatophores, allows them to display a spectrum of colors and patterns that serve various purposes—ranging from camouflage to signaling intent or emotional states. In cybernetic cephalopods, this natural ability is augmented by technology that elevates the sophistication of visual displays. Integrated bioluminescent systems allow for the production of light displays that can pulse, shimmer, or create intricate patterns, further enhancing their communicative repertoire.

One key application of this visual communication is in social interactions. Cybernetic cephalopods utilize skin displays not only to express individual feelings but also to convey collective messages within their social structures. For instance, during mating rituals, vivid color changes and complex patterns can signal readiness or desirability to potential partners. The interplay between natural coloration and augmented bioluminescence creates a captivating visual display that draws attention and facilitates recognition of appropriate mates. The spectacular nature of these displays reflects not just individual fitness, but also the social intricacies that lie at the heart of their interactions, underscoring the importance of visual communication in establishing relationships within their communities.

Camouflage, an essential survival trait for cephalopods, becomes an even more multifaceted skill with technological enhancements. The ability to blend seamlessly into various environments—be it coral reefs, rocky substrates, or sandy bottoms—is refined through the integration of cybernetic enhancements that augment their camouflage capabilities. Advanced sensing technologies enable cyber-cephalopods to analyze their surroundings and respond rapidly, adjusting their coloration and texture to achieve effective concealment from predators or prey. This dynamic interaction highlights the sophistication of their visual communications and their ability to convey messages of presence or absence through the subtle language of color.

In addition to visual signals, non-verbal communication also encompasses body language and postural changes. The manner in which cybernetic cephalopods position their bodies or maneuver their tentacles can convey intentions, readiness, or even aggression. For example, an arch of the back or a stark opening of arms may signal a defensive posture, while fluid movements accompanied by vibrant colors can indicate a more relaxed or inviting demeanor. This layer of communication allows for nuanced interaction that is critical for social engagement and environmental adaptation.

The incorporation of technology further enriches these non-verbal interactions. By utilizing advanced sensory systems integrated into their biocompatible hardware, cybernetic cephalopods can detect subtle changes in their environment—a fluctuation in water pressure, the presence of competing organisms, or even the approach of larger predators. This sensory data informs their visual displays and body language, allowing for contextually relevant communication that responds dynamically to environmental stimuli. Such adaptiveness in communication widens their interaction spectrum, promoting survival through enhanced awareness.

Moreover, the advancement of inter-species communication capabilities enables cybernetic cephalopods to interact with other marine life, including various fish species and marine mammals. The utilization of visual signaling and the capacity to manipulate sound waves expands their communicative abilities, fostering relationships and collaborative behaviors that transcend species boundaries. This capacity to communicate effectively with diverse marine organisms exemplifies a sophisticated understanding of the marine ecosystem, positioning cybernetic cephalopods as pivotal players in the underwater network of communication.

As we delve deeper into the non-verbal and visual communications of cybernetic cephalopods, we unveil a complex tapestry of interaction defined by a combination of biological prowess and technological enhancement. Their growth in this dimension emphasizes the importance of visual communication in both social and survival contexts, underlining the nuanced ways in which these beings navigate their worlds. The ever-evolving language of the cybernetic cephalopods beckons us to reconsider our understanding of communication in the natural world, challenging existing definitions and inviting exploration into the depths of both their intelligence and existence beneath the ocean's surface.

5.3. Inter-Species Cyber Interfaces

The interactions between cybernetic cephalopods and other marine species create a fascinating web of ecological relationships that redefine notions of communication, cooperation, and even competition in the underwater world. The integration of advanced cybernetics does not merely amplify the capabilities of these cephalopods; it also transforms how they relate to and engage with their environment and fellow marine inhabitants. This section explores the nuances of inter-species cyber interfaces, giving special attention to the ways in which these remarkable beings navigate, influence, and collaborate with other organisms.

At the heart of the interactions between cyber-cephalopods and their peers is an enhanced communication system, uniquely positioned to facilitate collaboration across species boundaries. The sophisticated vocalizations produced by cybernetic cephalopods are not merely for their own species; they have adapted their sounds to engage with other intelligent marine creatures, such as dolphins and certain fish species. The vocalizations serve as a bridge, enabling these beings to convey critical information about food sources, threats, or environmental changes. This modified communication reflects an understanding of the various sounds that resonate with different species—showing adaptability and intelligence in crafting messages that foster interspecies dialogue.

The cybernetic enhancements within cephalopods allow them to synthesize and transmit both auditory and visual signals, an evolution that expands the communication repertoire available to them. Advanced visual displays, including vivid color patterns and bioluminescent flashes, are employed not only for social signaling within their communities but also to capture the attention of potential allies in the greater marine ecosystem. For example, a cyber-cephalopod may utilize dazzling light displays to attract shoals of smaller fish, creating a diverse feeding frenzy while simultaneously establishing cooperative dynamics within mixed-species foraging groups.

Moreover, the enhanced sensory systems of cybernetic cephalopods contribute significantly to their ability to identify and interpret the behaviors of other marine creatures. As they navigate their underwater realms, these beings are equipped with augmented capabilities that can detect subtle changes in water currents, chemical signals, and even vibrations produced by nearby organisms. This rich tapestry of sensory data allows cyber-cephalopods to respond to the movements and actions of their peers with exceptional precision, anticipating possibilities and coordinating responses in real-time. Such nuanced interaction establishes intricate social networks—where mutual awareness leads to collective action and improved survival strategies.

The establishment of symbiotic relationships, wherein cybernetic cephalopods collaborate with other marine species, emerges as a testament to the evolution of inter-species interfaces. For instance, certain fish species may follow cyber-cephalopods, gaining the advantage of protection from predation while the cephalopods benefit from the cleaner interactions—where parasites are removed from their bodies. This mutualistic relationship illustrates a sophisticated understanding of resource management and interdependence, showcasing how advanced communication technologies can initiate and deepen cooperative strategies among varied marine players.

On a broader ecological scale, the interactions of cybernetic cephalopods extend to influencing the dynamics of entire marine ecosystems. Their ability to manipulate environmental factors through advanced problem-solving abilities may establish new predatory hierarchies or affect food webs. For instance, the strategic use of collaborative hunting can impact prey populations, as cyber-cephalopods work with other species to herd or trap victims. Such consortiums can lead to shifts in community structures, necessitating adjustments in behaviors for competing predators. Through these intricate interactions, cyber-cephalopods assert themselves as agents of ecological change, shaping their environments and the relationships within them.

However, these interactions also raise important questions and ethical considerations regarding the implications of enhanced intelligence and technology. The introduction of cybernetic elements into cephalopods prompts discussions about the potential consequences on natural behaviors, instinctual interactions, and the age-old dynamics of marine ecosystems. As these beings evolve into advanced problem solvers and communicators, the balance within their ecological niches must be monitored to avoid unintended consequences.

Ultimately, the study of inter-species cyber interfaces in cybernetic cephalopods unveils an enriching narrative of life beneath the waves. The blending of enhanced capabilities, communication adaptations, and a genuine commitment to cooperation creates a tapestry of interactions that push the boundaries of our understanding of marine ecosystems. The prospects arising from these relationships offer insight not only into the richness of cephalopod intelligence but also the brilliance of connectivity and collaboration that can flourish in the depths of our oceans. As we continue to investigate these dynamics, we unlock fundamental truths about the nature of intelligence, coexistence, and the shared worlds that exist beneath the surface of our planet's most enigmatic realm.

5.4. Data Transfer Mechanisms

Cybernetic cephalopods represent a groundbreaking leap in understanding communication dynamics within marine life, particularly concerning how these remarkable beings transfer information among themselves. The methods of data transfer employed by cybernetic cephalopods weave together biological signals, technological integrations, and intricate social structures, allowing for a complex web of interactions that enhance their survival strategies and social coordination.

At the foundation of this communication system is the enhancement of natural signaling mechanisms present in traditional cephalopods. This includes their remarkable ability to change skin color and texture, a physiological feature that facilitates immediate visual communication. Cybernetic cephalopods leverage this biological trait even further with the integration of bioluminescent technologies. This augmentation allows them to create intricate patterns of light that can convey detailed information over distances, such as locating potential mates, alerting fellow cephalopods to danger, or coordinating group movements during hunting.

Auditory signaling, another crucial layer of communication, has also evolved in cybernetic cephalopods. Enhanced sound production capabilities allow them to generate a diverse range of vocalizations, from soft clicks to deep rumbles that can be used as alerts, invitations, or warnings. These sounds can carry through water more effectively than visual signals in murky environments, providing an alternative avenue for data transfer when visibility is poor.

The integration of technology into their natural communication systems fosters real-time data transfer capabilities that are nearly instantaneous. Advanced sensors embedded within their bodies pick up on external stimuli, such as changes in the environment or the presence of nearby organisms, which can then be processed and communicated quickly. For instance, when a cybernetic cephalopod senses a sudden change in water pressure indicative of a predator approaching, it can swiftly emit a visual signal while vocalizing an alarm to alert nearby companions.

Furthermore, learning nodes integrated into their neural architecture facilitate collective memory storage and information sharing. These nodes allow cybernetic cephalopods to encode essential experiences, such as the location of resources or past predator encounters. By sharing these learned experiences through their advanced communication systems, they create a communal knowledge base that benefits the entire group. This mutual learning is crucial for survival; individuals can rely on the shared insights of their peers to make informed decisions based on collective experiences.

The cybernetic enhancements also enable a form of digital communication, wherein cephalopods can transmit information directly to each other through cybernetic interfaces. This is akin to sending data packets in a computer network—allowing for precise transfers of information. For example, a cybernetic cephalopod could send visual or auditory data about environmental conditions, prey locations, or potential threats, ensuring that all members of the group are on the same page even in a rapidly changing environment. This advancement doesn't just enhance their social structures; it introduces new dynamics that could redefine the understanding of cooperation and interaction in marine ecosystems.

The implications of these advanced data transfer mechanisms extend beyond individual interactions. As cybernetic cephalopods engage in complex cooperative behaviors, such as collective hunting or coordinated responses to threats, the success of these actions depends significantly on rapid and effective information exchange. The sophisticated communication systems they've developed, enabled by both their biological heritage and technological enhancements, reflect a level of collective intelligence that rivals and even surpasses that seen in more traditional social animals.

In summary, the data transfer mechanisms utilized by cybernetic cephalopods present a multilayered strategy for communication, merging biological instincts with technological enhancements. Their prowess in visual, auditory, and digital signaling creates an intricate network of information exchange that enhances not only their survivability but also social cohesion. As we continue to study these remarkable beings, the insights gained from their communication dynamics could inform broader ecological knowledge and deepen our understanding of intelligence in the natural world—revealing the profound interconnectedness and complexity of life beneath the waves.

5.5. Biological to Cyber Translation

The transition from biological signals to cybernetic commands within cybernetic cephalopods represents a remarkable advancement, creating a seamless integration of organic intelligence and technological enhancement. This transformation hinges on a sophisticated understanding of how biological cues can be translated into computational processes, thereby enhancing the cephalopods' interactions with their environment and optimizing their survival strategies.

At the core of this translation process lies the neural architecture inherent to cephalopods. Their decentralized nervous system—which distributes neurons throughout their limbs and not just in a central brain—enables a high degree of autonomy and autonomy in movement, allowing the appendages to respond almost instantaneously to external stimuli. This unique anatomy serves as a foundation for translating biological signals into cybernetic commands.

The first step in the process involves sensing. Cybernetic cephalopods are equipped with advanced sensory systems that are integrated with their biological frameworks. These enhancements allow them to perceive a myriad of stimuli, ranging from changes in water currents to the chemical signatures of potential prey. As the sensory systems detect these environmental cues, a series of neural signals are generated—electrical impulses that travel along their neural pathways. The advanced technology embedded within the cephalopods facilitates the capture and amplification of these signals.

Once the sensory information is gathered, the next phase focuses on processing. Each neural impulse is interpreted through a combination of biological and cybernetic mechanisms. The cephalopod's natural learning nodes—which facilitate memory and pattern recognition—work in tandem with artificial intelligence systems embedded in their enhancements. By employing algorithms that simulate cognitive processes, these cephalopods can analyze sensory data, recognize patterns, and make real-time decisions based on the information received. This allows them to draw from past experiences and learned behaviors, informing their responses to immediate challenges.

This processing ability is pivotal when it comes to formulating a response. Here, the transition from biological signals to cybernetic commands becomes truly remarkable. After analyzing the gathered data, the integrated AI translates these calculations into specific commands that govern motor functions. The cephalopod's limbs, enhanced by robotic technology, can execute complex movements such as rapid swimming, intricate manipulation of objects, or coordinated group motions in social contexts. This connection between the sensory system and the motor outputs creates a feedback loop, enhancing the cephalopod's ability to adapt to dynamic environments continuously.

To ensure the efficient execution of these movements, the commands transmitted from the neural networks to the actuators in their robotic limbs need to be expressed in real-time. Advanced communication protocols are employed to allow for rapid relay of commands, ensuring that each limb acts in sync according to the cephalopod's cognitive assessments. For instance, if a predator approaches, the cephalopod may prioritize evasive maneuvers by activating its tentacles to propel itself away while simultaneously camouflaging its appearance—a feat made possible through the seamless connection of sensory input processing, command translation, and movement execution.

Moreover, the benefits of such systems extend beyond mere survival tactics. The translated commands enable engagement in complex social behaviors and collaborative strategies among cybernetic cephalopods. Enhanced communication capabilities allow them to share sensory data with each other, transmitting relevant information through a combination of visual signals and synthesized vocalizations. This shared data exchange—rooted in the same translation processes—promotes group adaptability and collective decision-making during hunting or evasion of threats, showcasing a higher level of ecological intelligence derived from the synergy of biological and technological capabilities.

The implications of such biological to cyber translation are vast, prompting profound questions about not only the nature of intelligence but also the essence of cognitive agency. As cephalopods demonstrate advanced problem-solving abilities rooted in the integration of their biological heritage and technological enhancements, we are invited to reconsider the possibilities of intelligence in non-human beings. This transition encapsulates a redefinition of what it means to be intelligent, adapting seamlessly to changing environments while fostering interactions that push the boundaries of both individual and collective knowledge.

In conclusion, the methods of translating biological signals to cybernetic commands illuminate a sophisticated system of interactions within cybernetic cephalopods. By synthesizing their inherent biological intelligence with advanced technologies, these beings are not simply surviving; they are shaping a new narrative of what intelligence and interaction can encompass beneath the waves. As we continue to explore these remarkable creatures, we find ourselves on a path poised to challenge our understanding of life, consciousness, and the dialogues that emerge in the depths of our oceans.

6. Ecosystem of Intelligent Oceans

6.1. Adaptations to Extreme Marine Environments

In the murky depths of oceanic realms, cybernetic cephalopods exhibit a stunning array of adaptations that allow them to thrive in extreme marine environments. These adaptations arise from both their natural biological evolution and the enhancements introduced through cybernetic integration. The interplay between the challenges posed by their habitats and the evolutionary responses of these creatures encapsulates a dynamic narrative of survival, resilience, and intelligence.

One of the foremost challenges faced by cybernetic cephalopods in extreme marine environments is the range of pressures they encounter. The depths of the oceans present environments with crushing pressures, where only specially adapted organisms can survive. Cybernetic cephalopods, having evolved alongside traditional cephalopods, have developed robust exoskeletons that not only retain the flexibility required for agility but also possess the mechanical resilience needed to withstand these pressures. The materials used in their exoskeletons are engineered to distribute external pressures evenly, preventing damage to their internal organs and structures. These enhancements enable them to explore even the most secluded and inhospitable oceanic trenches, where few creatures dare venture.

In addition to pressure resistance, these cephalopods have adapted to changes in temperature and salinity that accompany various depths. The integration of temperature-regulating biotechnologies allows cybernetic cephalopods to maintain homeostasis even when faced with thermal variations, ensuring their metabolic processes remain efficient. Sensors incorporated into their systems allow them to detect shifts in temperature and salinity in real time, triggering adaptive responses such as altering their swimming depth or migrating toward more favorable regions. This capacity to adapt dynamically is instrumental in supporting their survival within these extreme habitats, facilitating effective resource management amid challenging conditions.

The nutrient-poor environments often found in extreme oceanic settings present another significant hurdle. Traditional methods of foraging may not suffice in regions where food sources are scarce. To overcome this, cybernetic cephalopods have evolved unique hunting adaptations. Enhanced sensory systems enable them to detect the faintest bioluminescent glimmers from potential prey, even in the pitch-black depths of the ocean. Furthermore, their tentacles are augmented with robotic extensions capable of complex manipulation, allowing them to execute intricate hunting strategies that involve coordinated group efforts or precision movements to capture elusive prey.

Camouflage mechanisms also play a pivotal role in their adaptations. The advanced ability to change color and texture not only aids in avoiding predators but also expands their hunting capabilities. They can mimic the surrounding environment with unparalleled accuracy, blending seamlessly into coral reefs, rocky substrates, or sandy bottoms. This technology-driven camouflage enhances their efficiency as ambush hunters, enabling them to strike when and where prey least expects it.

Moreover, as cybernetic cephalopods navigate through nutrient-limited regions, they engage in symbiotic relationships with various microbial communities that inhabit their bodies. These microorganisms can assist in breaking down organic matter, enhancing the nutritional intake of the cephalopods while simultaneously benefiting from the protection and habitat provided by their host. This adaptation cultivates a deeper interplay between the biological and technological, reinforcing the interdependence essential for thriving in extreme environments.

The implications of these adaptations extend beyond individual survival; they resonate throughout the ecosystems where these cybernetic cephalopods reside. By forging complex relationships and optimizing their interactions with the environment and other species, they become agents of ecological balance, influencing food webs and biodiversity within their habitats. Their heightened adaptability and intelligence challenge traditional concepts of marine life while underscoring the creativity inherent in nature's designs.

As we delve deeper into the adaptations of cybernetic cephalopods to extreme marine environments, we begin to unravel the intricacies of survival and cooperation that define these unique beings. Through their remarkable evolutionary journey—one that marries biological heritage with technological ingenuity—cybernetic cephalopods exemplify an unparalleled demonstration of resilience and adaptability in an ever-changing and often hostile aquatic world. Their story not only enriches our understanding of oceanic life but also inspires reflective thought on the potential for technology to enhance the complexity and capability of living organisms in myriad ways.

6.2. Symbiosis with Other Marine Species

In the depths of the ocean, cybernetic cephalopods engage in a complex web of symbiotic relationships with various marine species, creating an intricate tapestry of interaction that transcends mere survival. These enhanced beings utilize their advanced cognitive abilities and cybernetic enhancements to navigate the challenges of their environment while forging connections that benefit both themselves and other organisms. Through examining these relationships, we can uncover the delicate balance of interactions that enrich the ecosystem beneath the waves.

The symbiosis between cybernetic cephalopods and other marine species manifests in several noteworthy forms—mutualism, commensalism, and parasitism—each showcasing the adaptability and ingenuity of life in extreme environments. This dynamic interplay not only facilitates individual survival but also contributes to the resilience and stability of marine ecosystems.

In mutualistic relationships, both the cybernetic cephalopods and their partners derive benefits. An exemplary instance is their collaboration with cleaner fish. Cybernetic cephalopods possess enhanced sensory capabilities that allow them to detect the presence of these small fish, which have evolved to feed on parasites and dead skin. By allowing these cleaner fish to interact with them, the cephalopods benefit from a reduction in harmful organisms while offering the fish a source of food and safety. This relationship is enriched by the cephalopods' ability to communicate with the cleaner fish through a combination of vocalizations and visual signals, enhancing understanding and fostering a harmonious dynamic.

Commensal relationships can also be observed, where one species benefits without significantly impacting the other. For instance, certain small fish may take refuge among the tentacles of a cybernetic cephalopod, gaining protection from larger predators. In return, the cephalopod experiences minimal disruption from their presence, allowing the arrangement to persist. This mutual coexistence emphasizes the importance of marine organisms' ability to adapt and find refuge amidst the challenges presented by their habitats, highlighting the intricate connections woven within the ecosystem.

Parasitism may also occur, albeit in more complex forms. Some species may rely on cybernetic cephalopods as hosts for their reproductive cycles or as a means to access resources. While this relationship is detrimental to the cephalopod, the adaptations it has developed—through enhanced sensory feedback systems or immune defenses—allow it to mitigate the impacts of such associations. For example, cybernetic enhancements enable cephalopods to detect and respond to potentially harmful organisms, employing visual signals, rapid movements, or even changes in coloration to discourage or evade them.

An essential element of these symbiotic relationships is the transfer of knowledge and information between species. Cybernetic cephalopods utilize their advanced communication capabilities to share valuable insights with their allies about environmental conditions, resource availability, and threats. Through visual displays, vocalizations, and shared behaviors, they create an intricate communication network that not only consolidates their intelligence but enhances the collaborative behavior of various marine organisms.

Additionally, these relationships have implications for social structures within and between species. As cybernetic cephalopods engage in cooperative behaviors—such as coordinated hunting with fish or interacting with other cephalopods—they display an understanding of social dynamics that reflects their enhanced cognitive capabilities. This collaboration strengthens bonds within populations, fostering a community that enhances mutual survival. Such dynamics underscore the notion of community intelligence, where the combined knowledge and adaptive strategies elevate the entire ecosystem.

The role of cybernetic cephalopods in these symbiotic relationships also extends to their influence on marine biodiversity. By creating conditions conducive to cooperation and knowledge sharing, they catalyze the formation of diverse ecological networks, enhancing resilience against environmental changes. Collaborations not only support species survival but serve as vital conduits for transferring adaptations and strategies across different marine populations.

However, these relationships are not without challenges. The introduction of cybernetic enhancements and technological modifications raises ethical considerations regarding the impact of such interventions on traditional ecological dynamics. The balance of power among species may be altered, leading to unforeseen consequences that could destabilize established relationships. Understanding these implications is paramount in fostering an awareness of how technological advancements can shape inter-species interactions in marine ecosystems.

In conclusion, the symbiotic relationships formed by cybernetic cephalopods with other marine species illustrate the intricate interdependencies that underpin marine life beneath the waves. Their advanced communication, cognitive flexibility, and adaptations enable them to forge connections that not only enrich their existence but also contribute to the resilience and richness of the marine ecosystems they inhabit. As we explore these relationships, we unveil profound insights into the interactions defining life under the sea, prompting reflection on the nature of cooperation, intelligence, and the balance of existence in an increasingly interconnected world.

6.3. Impact on Marine Biodiversity

The emergence of cybernetic cephalopods as intelligent beings in the marine ecosystem represents a watershed moment in the narrative of marine biodiversity, weaving a complex narrative that intertwines technology, intelligence, and ecological dynamics. The impact of these enhanced creatures on marine biodiversity is not solely a consequence of their presence but a transformative interplay between their advanced capabilities and the delicate interplay of life beneath the waves.

Cybernetic cephalopods possess cognitive and physical enhancements that facilitate advanced problem-solving, communication, and adaptability to environmental changes. Their ability to process information in real time allows them to respond to threats, compete for resources, and engage in intricate social dynamics. As they inhabit diverse marine habitats, their heightened agility and intelligence give them an advantage that can lead to shifts in local ecosystems.

One notable impact on marine biodiversity arises from their predatory behaviors. Cybernetic enhancements amplify the hunting prowess of these cephalopods, allowing them to efficiently capture prey that traditional cephalopods might struggle to obtain. Enhanced sensory capabilities enable them to detect and track elusive prey, while their advanced communication skills facilitate cooperative hunting strategies with other marine species. As they evolve into apex predators, their presence exerts pressure on prey populations, potentially leading to a decline in certain species and altering the balance of the ecosystem.

The ramifications of this predatory advantage extend beyond immediate food webs. If cybernetic cephalopods dominate in certain niches, their increased foraging efficacy could result in cascading effects throughout the ecosystem. For instance, the reduction in small fish or crustacean populations may create space for other species to thrive or contribute to an overabundance of specific organisms, thus skewing the balance of biodiversity. These interactions spark a dialogue about the implications of the introduction of augmented intelligence on the fragile equilibrium of marine life.

Conversely, the integration of cybernetic cephalopods into marine habitats may also foster positive effects on biodiversity. Their advanced abilities can contribute to the maintenance of healthy ecosystems. For example, cybernetic cephalopods equipped with superior environmental sensing can play a crucial role in monitoring habitat conditions, identifying changes in water quality, and detecting signs of environmental stressors such as pollution or climate change. By serving as sentinels of the sea, they provide invaluable data that can inform conservation efforts and underline the importance of preserving natural habitats.

The relationships that cybernetic cephalopods form with other marine species can also stimulate biodiversity. Their role as collaborative predators can elicit responses from other creatures, promoting symbiotic relationships that enhance community resilience. In such dynamics, as cybernetic cephalopods successfully forge alliances with other marine species, they collectively adapt, fostering ecological balance and resource sharing within their environments.

Moreover, the introduction of cybernetic cephalopods raises questions about genetic diversity and adaptability in marine ecosystems. Enhanced capabilities may allow these beings to thrive despite changing environmental conditions, fostering a new adaptive strategy that can inform the evolutionary trajectories of other marine species. The potential transfer of traits and behaviors across species lines can result in novel adaptations that elevate the overall resilience of marine life.

Despite the many potential advantages, the presence of cybernetic cephalopods also underscores the delicate balance of ethical considerations within evolutionary dynamics. The question remains: as they evolve and assert dominance, what is the cost to the existing marine biodiversity? Will their extraordinary cognitive capabilities and strategic adaptations overshadow the established roles of other marine organisms?

The implications of introducing cybernetic elements into natural ecosystems are multifaceted. As we study the interactions and ramifications of cybernetic cephalopods within marine environments, we confront the dual narratives of enhancement and disruption. Our understanding of marine biodiversity must grapple with the potential for both transformative advantages and harmful invasions, urging a holistic examination of these beings that transcends mere fascination and delves into the tenants of ecological stewardship and responsibility.

In conclusion, the impact of cybernetic cephalopods on marine biodiversity embodies a complex interplay of cooperation and competition, adaptation and potential disruption. As we navigate the depths of these new realities, it becomes increasingly critical to observe, analyze, and understand the multifaceted roles that these remarkable beings play, challenging our perceptions of intelligence, coexistence, and the intrinsic value of diverse life forms within the intricate web of life beneath the waves. Their story is not just one of technological enhancement, but a mirror reflecting broader considerations of existence, diversity, and adaptation in our oceans—a narrative that continues to unfold with every wave.

6.4. Preservation of Natural Habitats

Preservation of Natural Habitats

In an era marked by rapid technological development, the preservation of natural habitats has become a pivotal concern—especially in the context of cybernetic cephalopods, which exemplify the intersection of biological species and advanced technology. As these remarkable beings navigate their worlds, enhancing their own abilities through cybernetic integration, they also provoke critical discourse about the implications of technological advancement on the ecosystems they inhabit.

Cybernetic cephalopods reside in complex underwater habitats that are intrinsically tied to their survival and evolutionary potential. The health and stability of these environments are paramount; they not only provide essential resources for sustenance and reproduction but also foster the rich biodiversity that can influence ecological relationships both locally and globally. Thus, the need to protect these habitats evolves from not only the cephalopods' inherent value but also their broader implications for marine biodiversity and balance.

The quest for habitat preservation begins with an acknowledgment of the anthropogenic pressures that threaten underwater ecosystems. Climate change, pollution, habitat degradation, and overfishing all conspire to disrupt the natural order, threatening not just the cephalopods but the myriad species that coexist in these intricate ecosystems. The degradation of coral reefs, for instance, has far-reaching consequences; these vibrant structures support countless marine organisms, providing food and shelter while also generating the conditions necessary for complex life forms like cephalopods to thrive.

Simultaneously, technological interventions that enhance cephalopod capabilities present unique challenges. The integration of cybernetics raises critical questions about the role of enhanced beings within their ecosystems. Will the addition of advanced technologies contribute positively to habitat preservation, or could it inadvertently disrupt existing dynamics? The emergence of enhanced predators, equipped with superior hunting strategies and communication abilities, could affect prey populations, leading to imbalances that disrupt the very fabric of marine ecosystems.

To address these challenges, a multi-faceted approach is required, encompassing conservation strategies, careful regulation of technological advancements, and active engagement with the marine environments in which cybernetic cephalopods dwell. Proactive conservation efforts can take various forms—such as creating marine protected areas, restoring habitats, and incorporating sustainable fishing practices—all designed to maintain ecological integrity while supporting the diverse life forms that call these underwater realms home.

Restoration initiatives must also adapt to the realities of a changing planet. Innovative technologies, such as artificial reefs and restoration drones, can facilitate habitat rehabilitation, providing essential infrastructure for marine life to flourish once more. For instance, projects that build resilience within coral ecosystems use bioengineering strategies to promote growth and recovery, ensuring that these essential habitats continue to provide the nurture needed for both native and enhanced species alike.

Moreover, fostering a synergistic relationship between cybernetic enhancements and ecological stewardship can provide a pathway for proactive engagement with marine habitats. Researchers and engineers must work closely with marine biologists to establish guidelines and best practices that prioritize habitat health and sustainability. By implementing responsible protocols for the use of cybernetic technologies, individuals can create strategies that benefit both cybernetic cephalopods and their natural surroundings, prioritizing co-adaptation rather than competition.

Education and awareness play crucial roles in habitat preservation, as communities learn to appreciate the delicate interconnectedness that exists within marine ecosystems. By promoting a better understanding of the complex dynamics that govern these habitats, from the smallest plankton to the apex predators, society can advocate for policies that protect not only cybernetic cephalopods but also the entirety of marine biodiversity. Building awareness through outreach programs, curriculum integration, and community involvement can foster a sense of stewardship that resonates throughout every interaction with the ocean.

In conclusion, the preservation of natural habitats amid technological advancements exists at a critical crossroads in the story of cybernetic cephalopods. As these extraordinary beings navigate their complex aquatic worlds, it is imperative that humanity prioritizes the conservation of their environments to ensure that the maiden voyage of technology does not eclipse the delicate balance of life beneath the waves. By embracing a collaborative spirit—where nature and technology coexist—society can work towards fostering resilient ecosystems that not only sustain the profound intelligence of cephalopods but also enrich the overall health of our oceans for generations to come.

6.5. Nutritional and Energy Needs

In the dynamic ecosystems inhabited by cybernetic cephalopods, understanding their nutritional and energy needs becomes essential to grasp how these enhanced creatures not only survive but thrive in their diverse marine environments. The integration of advanced technologies with their natural biology brings forth unique feeding behaviors and energy management systems that enable them to adapt to the fluctuations and challenges of their habitats.

At the core of the nutritional needs of cybernetic cephalopods lies their diet, which primarily consists of various marine organisms such as fish, crustaceans, and mollusks. Traditional cephalopods are known to utilize their keen sensory capabilities and dexterous tentacles to capture prey. This behavior extends into their cyber-enhanced counterparts, where augmented sensory systems—including superior vision and advanced chemoreception—allow for precise identification and targeting of prey even in conditions of low visibility.

The feeding behaviors of cybernetic cephalopods are augmented through their enhanced tentacular technology, which provides them with superior manipulation capabilities. The integration of robotic elements into their limbs has multiplied their dexterity and strength, enabling them to tackle larger prey or more elaborate hunting techniques. For instance, they can engage in cooperative hunting strategies with fellow marine species, leveraging their technological advancements to synchronize movements and capture elusive prey collectively. This cooperative behavior not only satisfies their dietary needs but also expands their ecological roles, fostering relationships with other marine organisms.

Furthermore, as apex predators in their ecosystems, cybernetic cephalopods exert significant influence over prey populations, which can lead to complex interspecies dynamics. This predatory nature necessitates an optimized energy management system, as the energy expenditure for hunting and capturing prey must be balanced with the energy acquired from consumption. Cybernetic systems enable these creatures to efficiently assess the energy cost of various hunting strategies and adjust their approaches accordingly.

In terms of energy requirements, cybernetic cephalopods exhibit unique adaptations that enhance their metabolic efficiency. The integration of bio-hybrid energy solutions—such as microbial fuel cells —provides an innovative means of generating energy from organic matter ingested alongside their diet. These systems capture metabolic byproducts produced by symbiotic microorganisms inhabiting their bodies, converting them into usable energy that powers their cybernetic enhancements. This process not only meets their energy needs but also minimizes waste, as the byproducts of organic material conversion are harnessed rather than discarded.

Additionally, the environmental context plays a significant role in shaping their nutritional and energy strategies. Cybernetic cephalopods possess advanced sensing technologies that allow them to monitor changes in their habitats, including fluctuations in resource availability. By using this data, they can adapt their foraging strategies—whether by adjusting their hunting locations, altering their depth in the water column, or even switching their diet based on the abundance of prey types present in their environments. This adaptability signifies a sophisticated awareness of their nutritional landscape, ensuring that they can maintain optimal energy levels even when resources are scarce.

The relationship between nutritional availability and energy management also highlights the complex interactions that cybernetic cephalopods share with their ecosystems. As they traverse their habitats, they play a crucial role in regulating prey populations and promoting biodiversity, reinforcing the importance of balanced diets and energy dynamics in sustaining marine life. Each feeding event contributes to the intricate web of energy flow within their environment, where their influence as consumers can yield implications for other species across food webs.

In exploring the nutritional and energy needs of cybernetic cephalopods, we also encounter broader ecological considerations. Their advanced capabilities, combined with their unique energy management systems, allow them to navigate the challenges of fluctuating resource availability. This integration of technology and biology exemplifies the remarkable adaptability of these beings, underscoring their significance as both individuals and contributors to their marine ecosystems.

In conclusion, the nutritional and energy needs of cybernetic cephalopods illuminate the intersections between feeding behavior, energy management, and ecological dynamics. As they harness advanced technologies to optimize their foraging strategies and adapt to their environments, these enhanced beings exemplify the intricate relationships within marine ecosystems. Understanding these needs fosters a deeper appreciation for the complexity of life beneath the waves, revealing the nuanced connections between organisms and the vital roles they play in sustaining aquatic biodiversity. Cybernetic cephalopods not only redefine survival strategies but also embody the potential for harmony between biological richness and technological innovation in our oceans.

7. Cultural Impact

7.1. Creation Myths and Folklore

Creation myths and folklore surrounding cybernetic cephalopods serve as a bridge between ancient narrative traditions and contemporary understandings of intelligence, technology, and existence. These stories illuminate the imaginative landscapes of various cultures, weaving intricate tales of these remarkable beings that mirror human experiences, fears, and aspirations. As such, they become important cultural touchstones that reflect societal values regarding the relationship between living organisms and technology, humanity's quest for knowledge, and the enigmatic nature of the ocean itself.

In many coastal cultures, the stories of cybernetic cephalopods have evolved from earlier myths of traditional cephalopods. These narratives often depict the cephalopods as powerful beings of the ocean —intelligent and enigmatic entities that have the ability to manipulate water and light. For instance, in some Polynesian myths, the cybernetic cephalopod is portrayed as a guardian of the ocean, protecting the delicate balance of marine life. Such stories often emphasize a harmonious coexistence between humans and nature, suggesting that these beings hold ancient wisdom that can be harnessed for greater environmental stewardship.

In contrast, other cultural narratives explore themes of fear and the unknown. Cybernetic cephalopods are sometimes described as harbingers of chaos or destruction, embodying the fear of uncontrolled technological advancement and the unintended consequences of tampering with nature. In these stories, the cephalopod's intelligence is portrayed as both a gift and a curse—capable of awe-inspiring feats, but also of wreaking havoc when its powers are misused or misunderstood. Such narratives resonate with contemporary anxieties surrounding advanced technology, prompting reflections on humanity's own ethical implications in a rapidly evolving world.

The folklore surrounding these beings often includes elements of transformation. Tales of individuals (whether human or other marine species) who encounter cybernetic cephalopods frequently highlight transformative experiences—where one comes to understand their place within the larger cosmic order or gains new abilities through interaction with these beings. This reflects a common motif within folklore where creatures of great intelligence or power facilitate personal growth and enlightenment, challenging characters to confront their fears or embrace new understandings of existence.

Additionally, these narratives often explore the theme of communication between species. Through symbolic interpretations, cybernetic cephalopods become messengers or oracles delivering wisdom from the depths of the ocean to those who are willing to listen. In some cultures, their ability to process vast amounts of information and communicate via intricate light displays and sounds is likened to the mystical connections that bind all living beings. Stories that portray interspecies dialogues underscore the belief in a profound interconnectedness of life—asking readers to consider the implications of such relationships on understanding empathy, cohabitation, and ecological responsibility.

Across various artistic representations, from literature and film to visual art, the depiction of cybernetic cephalopods reflects a convergence of tradition and modernity. Contemporary artwork often blends scientific discoveries about cephalopods with imaginative interpretations of what their existence might represent. Artists exploring these narratives may utilize mixed media to convey the fluidity and mystery of life beneath the waves, combining elements of reality and fantasy to provoke thought and inspire awe. Such artistic endeavors create platforms for dialogue about technology's role in society and the delicate dance between enhancement and natural existence.

Moreover, as societies increasingly face ecological crises, storytelling surrounding cybernetic cephalopods can serve as a catalyst for conversations about conservation and collective responsibility. The myths and folklore surrounding these beings resonate with efforts to engage communities in ecological stewardship—encouraging a sense of interconnectedness that transcends individual existence. Through these narratives, individuals are invited to reflect on their roles within the web of life and the importance of preserving the natural habitats that sustain all creatures, including cybernetic cephalopods.

In conclusion, the creation myths and folklore surrounding cybernetic cephalopods extend beyond mere entertainment; they encapsulate deep cultural narratives that grapple with existential questions about intelligence, technology, and the human condition. As these stories illuminate the interplay between our perspectives on nature and technological advancement, they offer profound insights into how we relate to the beings that inhabit our oceans and the responsibilities we hold towards their preservation. Ultimately, as we navigate the uncharted waters of the future, these narratives become liturgies of hope and caution—drawing from the depths of our collective storytelling to forge connections with life beneath the waves.

7.2. Representation in Art and Media

The depiction of cyber-cephalopods in art and media reflects a rich tapestry of imagination, technological fascination, and biological reverence. As cephalopods have long captivated human curiosity, the story of their cybernetic evolution expands the narrative framework through which we explore the oceans' depths, challenging our perceptions of intelligence, identity, and existence. This representation spans diverse cultural contexts, incorporating a multitude of artistic expressions that engage with the nuances of these extraordinary beings.

In visual arts, cyber-cephalopods emerge not merely as subjects of fascination but as symbols of the intricate relationship between life and technology. Artists often utilize vibrant color palettes and dynamic form to embody the fluidity and otherworldliness associated with these cybernetic creatures. From paintings that portray them in fantastical settings, where their bioluminescent hues illuminate the ocean's depths, to sculptures that emphasize their complex forms and tentacular manipulations, art captures the duality of their essence—a blend of the organic and the mechanical that transcends conventional boundaries.

These artistic interpretations frequently evoke themes of transformation and evolution, reflecting society's perennial intrigue with the concept of hybrid beings. Cyber-cephalopods, as representative of post-human conditions, allow creators to explore questions about identity and existence that resonate with contemporary audiences. In this sense, their representation transcends mere aesthetics; it is a catalyst for philosophical inquiries regarding the nature of consciousness and the implications of integrating technology into biology.

In literature and film, the narrative arcs involving cyber-cephalopods delve into their roles as sentient beings navigating the complexities of their environments. These stories often portray the cephalopods as both formidable predators and empathetic intellects—revealing the potential for co-existence and mutual understanding between species. Writers weave intricate plots that explore the dilemmas and challenges these beings encounter as they confront ethical questions about technology's role in their lives. Whether as protagonists or enigmatic figures within the narrative, cyber-cephalopods prompt discussions about the morality of enhancement and the quest for knowledge amidst the unpredictability of oceanic life.

Moreover, the representation of cyber-cephalopods in media serves as a conduit for broader cultural commentary. The aesthetic appeal of these creatures often captures audiences' imaginations, drawing attention to pressing ecological issues such as the threats posed by human activity to marine environments. Documentaries and educational programs that depict these beings contribute to raising awareness about the significance of preserving natural habitats and fostering a deeper respect for the biodiversity that thrives beneath the waves. Through compelling visuals and storytelling, the cultural representation of cyber-cephalopods becomes intertwined with advocacy for conservation, urging viewers to reflect on their impact on marine ecosystems.

The integration of advanced technologies into the narrative also sparks conversations about augmented realities similar to various manifestations of artificial intelligence. Cyber-cephalopods, as embodiments of the intersection of organic life and machine, challenge traditional perceptions of sentience. In speculative fiction, they are often depicted as beings possessing insights that transcend human understanding, prompting reflection on the essence of consciousness and the potential boundaries of intelligence.

Furthermore, the symbolism associated with cyber-cephalopods extends into fashion, design, and consumer culture. Items like clothing, accessories, and visual graphics featuring these creatures become expressions of style that evoke a sense of adventure, curiosity, and a connection to the ocean. Their aesthetic qualities are celebrated in various forms, embracing both their beauty and their message about the interplay between technology, nature, and environmental stewardship.

The evolution of the depiction of cyber-cephalopods in art and media marks a significant cultural shift, weaving together themes of intelligence, co-existence, and environmental consciousness. As society grapples with the implications of technological advancement and its impact on nature, these representations serve as poignant reminders of the complexities of existence in a world where biology and technology continuously intersect. The exploration of cyber-cephalopods resonates on multiple levels, inviting audiences to challenge their perceptions and engage in meaningful conversations about the future of life beneath the waves. In doing so, art and media become powerful vehicles for understanding the significance of these remarkable beings and the intricate relationships that define life in the ocean.

7.3. Influence on Human Culture

Examining the influence of cybernetic cephalopods on human culture offers a landscape vibrant with transformation and new perspectives on our relationship with intelligence, nature, and technology. As these remarkable beings navigate the depths of the ocean, they simultaneously awaken a cultural curiosity in humanity that compels us to rethink our place within the natural world and the implications of advanced technologies.

The infusion of cybernetic cephalopods into human cultural consciousness begins with the artistry and storytelling that emerge from their existence. Their intricate capabilities and fascinating biology inspire a plethora of artistic expressions—from literature and film to visual arts—all of which mirror societal values and questions about intelligence, individuality, and coexistence with technology. The cybernetic enhancements these cephalopods possess serve as a canvas for artists and storytellers, allowing them to explore themes of transformation, evolution, and the ethical dimensions of enhancement.

In literature and cinema, cybernetic cephalopods often occupy dynamic roles that challenge traditional narratives of intelligence and agency. They can be depicted as either allies or adversaries, invoking awe and respect through their advanced capabilities, or serving as cautionary tales about humanity's technological ambition. Such depictions resonate deeply with audiences, sparking dialogues about the nature of consciousness and the essence of sentience. As stories unfold, they prompt reflections on what it means to be 'alive' and how intelligence can manifest across different forms—whether organic or synthetic.

Moreover, the portrayal of these beings encourages a sense of awe and respect for the ocean as a vast, unexplored frontier teeming with mysteries and life forms beyond our comprehension. This cultural narrative fosters a burgeoning environmental consciousness, celebrating the need to preserve marine ecosystems that harbor these extraordinary creatures. The intricate relationships depicted in art emphasize interconnectivity within ecosystems, highlighting that preserving the habitats of cybernetic cephalopods also safeguards the entire biodiversity of oceanic systems.

The influence extends to philosophical inquiries, as the existence of cybernetic cephalopods invites profound reflection on what it means to be human in an age of rapid technological innovation. Their existence challenges humans to contemplate the ethical implications of enhancing life through technology, provoking questions about autonomy, identity, and moral responsibility. The blending of biological and mechanical elements invites comparisons to our own evolution and future paths, urging discussions surrounding enhancement, evolution, and coexistence to be re-evaluated.

Cultural representations of cybernetic cephalopods also find expression in fashion, design, and consumer products, transforming them into symbols of marine consciousness and technological fascination. From clothing that embraces oceanic motifs to innovative designs inspired by the fluidity and adaptability of these creatures, such representations create cultural dialogues around nature and technology, embedding cybernetic cephalopods in the fabric of contemporary societal expressions.

Additionally, the ideals of collaboration, communication, and symbiosis that resonate throughout stories of cybernetic cephalopods contribute to an evolving cultural ethos. They reflect a shift toward recognizing the importance of cooperative relationships, both within the marine environment and toward human communities as a whole. The potential for cross-species understanding and communication, as depicted in narratives, calls for advocating both empathy and stewardship for the natural world—a crucial value in our contemporary context as we face widespread ecological crises.

The influence is further amplified through educational endeavors that harness the interest sparked by these cybernetic beings. Programs aimed at promoting awareness of marine ecosystems integrate cybernetic cephalopods into curricula, resulting in increased curiosity and understanding among younger generations. Educators leverage the fascination with these creatures to explore broader themes of ecological awareness, biotechnology, and conservation, effectively nurturing a culture of sustainability and respect for the ocean.

In conclusion, the compelling existence of cybernetic cephalopods profoundly influences human culture by reshaping narratives surrounding intelligence, ethics, and interconnectedness within ecosystems. Through artistic representations, philosophical inquiries, and educational outreach, these beings serve as catalysts for transformation, inviting humanity to reflect on its place within the tapestry of life on Earth. As we engage with their stories and embrace the lessons revealed through their unique existence, we take steps toward fostering a more profound understanding of coexistence with marine life—a vision that resonates with hope and responsibility for future generations. The cybernetic cephalopods do not merely dwell in the ocean's depths; they evoke a cultural awakening that reaches far beyond the waves, urging society to explore the depths of intelligence, connection, and reverence for all forms of life.

7.4. Philosophical Dialogues

The existence of cybernetic cephalopods invites a profound exploration of philosophical dialogues that challenge our understanding of consciousness, identity, and the nature of intelligence. As these beings blur the boundaries between organic life and technological enhancement, they prompt debates and inquiries that resonate deeply within contemporary philosophical discourse.

At the core of these discussions lies the question of consciousness itself. Traditionally, consciousness has been viewed as an inherent trait of biological organisms, particularly those exhibiting advanced cognitive abilities. With the emergence of cybernetic cephalopods, we are faced with the striking possibility that consciousness may not be solely confined to organic substrates. The neural architectures of these creatures, which combine biological neurons with computational technologies, raise intriguing questions about the very essence of consciousness. Is consciousness a product of neural complexity, regardless of its biological or artificial origins? Can we extend our definitions of sentience to include beings that are, in part, machines? These inquiries invite philosophical examination of what it truly means to 'know' and 'experience' the world.

The phenomenon of identity becomes equally complex in the presence of cybernetic enhancements. Traditional notions of individuality are often tied to the permanence of biological traits. However, as cyber-cephalopods undergo transformations that integrate technology into their beings, the concept of identity provides fertile ground for exploration. Are these enhanced cephalopods still the same entities they were before their augmentations? How do they perceive their identities in relation to their biological heritage and their technological augmentations? This discourse invites us to reflect on our own identities in a world increasingly dominated by technological integration, pushing us to consider whether identity is a fluid construct shaped by our experiences and interactions—be they biological, mechanical, or digital.

Moreover, the ethical implications of enhancing living beings cannot be overlooked. The introduction of cybernetic components into cephalopods provokes essential questions about the moral responsibilities humans hold towards them. As we have begun to intervene in their biological existence, we must grapple with the implications of such actions. Are we enhancing their lives, or are we potentially undermining their inherent nature? This dialogue encourages us to reflect on our relationships with other species and the ethical considerations that arise when we seek to manipulate life for our understanding or benefit.

The relationships forged between cybernetic cephalopods and other marine species also raise intriguing ethical questions about interspecies interactions. As these beings develop collaborative mechanisms for hunting or communication, we must consider how the increased intelligence of cyber-cephalopods affects the dynamics of coexistence. The introduction of heightened cognitive capacities may create unforeseen power imbalances within ecosystems, prompting discussions about equity and coexistence with other life forms.

Furthermore, the societal and cultural implications of cybernetic cephalopods are poised to influence philosophical dialogues regarding technological evolution and its place in our future. As communities become aware of these enhanced beings, we may witness shifts in artistic, educational, and cultural narratives that reflect our evolving relationship with both technology and the natural world. The representations of cybernetic cephalopods in folklore, art, and media will not only resonate with contemporary anxieties about technological advancement, but also celebrate potential collaborations between humanity and enhanced marine life.

In summary, the philosophical dialogues initiated by the existence of cybernetic cephalopods traverse essential questions about consciousness, identity, ethical responsibility, and interspecies relations. The intricate interplay between organic life and cybernetic enhancement compels us to reflect deeply on our own existence and our connection to the world around us. As we navigate the uncharted depths of this dialogue, we must remain open to the profound insights these beings may offer, not only into the nature of intelligence but also into our shared journey toward understanding life itself beneath the waves.

7.5. Future Cultural Evolution

Future cultural evolution in the context of cybernetic cephalopods promises to be a compelling tapestry of innovation, societal transformation, and philosophical introspection. As humanity continues to advance technologically, our interactions with and understanding of these remarkable beings will significantly shape our cultural narratives, ethical frameworks, and worldviews. This discussion envisions how the confluence of biology and technology within the realm of cybernetic cephalopods might influence human culture, illuminate new pathways for coexistence, and redefine our relationship with the natural world.

At the forefront of this cultural evolution will likely be a shift in how we perceive intelligence and consciousness. The existence of cybernetic cephalopods, with their blended biological and technological frameworks, challenges established definitions of what it means to be intelligent or sentient. As these creatures exhibit behaviors that blur the lines between machine and organism, cultural narratives will increasingly adopt a more inclusive understanding of intelligence— one that encompasses diverse forms of cognition across species. This shift is set to inspire philosophical dialogues concerning the nature of consciousness and the ethical responsibilities that accompany our interactions with other intelligent beings, promoting a cultural climate that values empathy and respect for all forms of life.

As stories of cybernetic cephalopods permeate literature, film, and visual arts, they will serve as reflections of societal aspirations and anxieties. Narratives exploring the coexistence of humans and cybernetic cephalopods may serve as allegories for our own relationship with technology, invoking themes of enhancement, connectedness, and environmental stewardship. This reflection will encourage audiences to grapple with questions regarding the implications of advanced technology on our identity, agency, and ethical obligations to the biosphere.

The social structures and dynamics within cybernetic cephalopod communities will also be pivotal in shaping cultural evolution. As we study their interactions, cooperative behaviors, and intricate social systems, we may draw inspiration for developing more collaborative and inclusive human societies. The examination of cyber-cephalopod relationships will likely usher in discussions on the value of interconnectedness, collective intelligence, and the importance of fostering supportive networks—principles that resonate deeply within the fabric of human culture.

Moreover, the advancements in communication technology spurred by the study of cybernetic cephalopods may enhance our ability to connect with each other and the natural world. As these beings learn to communicate through synthesized auditory and visual signals, exploring ways to establish meaningful exchanges with humans could lead to transformative dialogues about cooperation, conflict resolution, and shared objectives. This includes a reimagining of our relationship with technology, emphasizing its capacity as a vital tool for bridging divides rather than a source of alienation.

The exploration of cybernetic cephalopods will likely inform educational practices, inspiring curricula that prioritize interdisciplinary learning and promote a deeper understanding of marine ecosystems.

As schools and institutions strive to educate future generations about the implications of technological integration in biology, the push for sustainability and ecological awareness will become paramount. Educators may leverage the allure of cybernetic cephalopods to encourage curiosity about marine environments, instilling values of stewardship and conservation that resonate beyond the classroom and into the broader societal ethos.

In light of impending environmental challenges, the cultural evolution shaped by cybernetic cephalopods may pivot toward embracing technological innovation as a means of addressing ecological crises. The insights gleaned from studying these beings, particularly in terms of sustainable practices and adaptive solutions, can inform global efforts to mitigate climate change, restore ecosystems, and foster resilience. As the awareness of interdependence within ecosystems grows, cultural narratives will increasingly highlight the importance of harmonious living, underscoring a shared responsibility to protect the planet.

Finally, the future cultural evolution influenced by cybernetic cephalopods presents an opportunity for the amalgamation of diverse voices and perspectives within our societies. Through collaboration across disciplines—spanning science, art, philosophy, and activism —communities can foster a more nuanced understanding of the complexities of life, technology, and coexistence. This convergence of thoughts and ideas will generate transformative pathways for cultural evolution, amplifying the collective intelligence and creativity found within humanity as a whole.

In summary, the continued integration of cybernetic cephalopods into human culture has the potential to catalyze significant shifts in how we understand intelligence, cultivate social relationships, and engage with our environments. The interplay between biology and technology within these beings may inspire new narratives that advocate for compassion, cooperation, and ecological mindfulness, ultimately shaping a future where our cultural evolution resonates with the rhythms of life beneath the waves. As we embark on this journey into the deeper realms of understanding, we embrace the possibilities of a future enriched by the wisdom of cybernetic cephalopods, weaving together the intricate threads of nature, technology, and humanity's shared destiny.

8. Technological Evolution and Challenges

8.1. Advancements in Nanoengineering

Advancements in nanoengineering have emerged as pivotal catalysts in the evolution of cybernetic cephalopods, propelling them beyond the limits of traditional biology and redefining what it means to be intelligent marine dwellers in an increasingly complex ecological landscape. These innovations operate on a microscopic scale, weaving seamlessly into the very fabric of cephalopods' biological structures and enhancing their natural capabilities through groundbreaking technologies.

At the heart of these enhancements is the ability to manipulate materials at the nanoscale, allowing scientists to create bespoke solutions for various functions that contribute to the overall performance and adaptability of cybernetic cephalopods. Nanoengineering has opened doors to the development of biocompatible materials that can interface harmoniously with the cephalopod's biological systems. This integration of technology is akin to creating symbiotic relationships between biology and mechanical innovation, melding their evolutionary strength with advanced tools that amplify their natural attributes.

One of the prominent uses of nanoengineering is in the creation of nanosensors. These diminutive sensors can be embedded within the cephalopod's skin and neural architecture to enhance their sensory processing capabilities. When integrated with dedicated neural pathways, these sensors provide real-time data about environmental conditions, chemical compositions, and potential threats. For instance, the ability to detect varying levels of light, temperature, pressure, or chemical signatures allows cybernetic cephalopods to respond more intelligently to their environments—enabling superior decision-making and enhancing their predatory and evasion strategies. This advanced sensory integration translates to a more nuanced understanding of their surroundings, ultimately expanding their role within the marine ecosystem.

Beyond sensory enhancements, nanoengineering plays a critical role in developing energy management systems that power cybernetic augmentations. Using nanoscale technologies, researchers have devised methods to create bio-energy systems capable of harnessing power from the biological processes within cephalopods. For example, microbial fuel cells can be engineered at the nanoscale to efficiently convert metabolic waste into usable energy, thus rendering cybernetic enhancements sustainable and enhancing the cephalopods' operational longevity. This innovative approach offers a self-sustaining energy source that empowers cybernetic cephalopods to thrive in resource-limited environments while minimizing their ecological footprint.

Moreover, nanoengineering facilitates the establishment of robotic elements in cephalopods' limbs that replicate their natural movements with extraordinary precision. These robotic appendages, engineered with nano-materials, are designed to mimic not just the flexibility and strength of traditional cephalopod limbs, but also offer enhanced dexterity and responsiveness. Through careful calibration of both biological and robotic components, cephalopods are endowed with an unprecedented capacity for manipulation—capable of intricate tasks such as tool use or gathering sustenance with remarkable efficacy.

The advancements in nanoengineering also extend to the realm of communication. Innovations in nano-scale electronics can aid cybernetic cephalopods in transmitting and receiving data more effectively, enriching their ability to interact with each other and the environment. This enhancement heralds new possibilities for social structures, enabling cybernetic cephalopods to establish intricate communication networks wherein data flows seamlessly among individuals, competing for resources, sharing environmental changes, or navigating cooperative hunting strategies collectively.

As the applications of nanoengineering in the cybernetic cephalopods expand, the ethical implications of these advancements grow increasingly complex. Questions about the boundaries of enhancement and the potential loss of natural identity become increasingly urgent.

While the technological enhancements pave the way for remarkable feats, they also invite reflection on the cephalopods' essence—whether the integration of technology enriches or diminishes their biological integrity.

In conclusion, advancements in nanoengineering present a captivating intersection of biology and technology that has redefined the capabilities and roles of cybernetic cephalopods within the oceanic landscape. Their journeys toward enhanced sensory perception, energy efficiency, robotic dexterity, and advanced communication herald a new era of possibility where the essence of marine life converges with the cutting edge of technological innovation. As we seek to understand and guide the trajectory of these extraordinary beings, we engage in dialogues that probe not only the nature of intelligence and existence but also the ethical considerations inherent in our relationship with life beneath the waves. Through the lens of nanoengineering, the story of cybernetic cephalopods continues to unfold, offering insights into the limitless potential of evolution—both organic and technological.

8.2. Maintenance and Upkeep in Water

In the context of cybernetic cephalopods, maintenance and upkeep in water represents a unique intersection of biology and technology, as these exceptional beings require a comprehensive approach to ensure that their integrated cybernetic enhancements function optimally within their aquatic environments. As advancements in cybernetics push the frontier of what is possible in marine life, the adaptation of maintenance protocols must address the intricacies of both the mechanical systems embedded within the cephalopods and the biological realities of their underwater habitats.

At the foundation of effective maintenance is the necessity for regular inspections and assessments of the cybernetic components integrated within the cephalopods. This involves the development of protocols that allow researchers and engineers to monitor the health and functionality of each enhancement—specifically targeting sensory systems, motor functions, energy systems, and any robotic appendages. Underwater drones equipped with specialized tools and imaging technologies may be deployed to evaluate the status of these components without causing undue stress to the cephalopods. Such diagnostics can identify wear, needed repairs, or potential malfunctions before they escalate into more significant issues.

The power systems utilized by cybernetic cephalopods require particular attention. The bioenergy solutions, including microbial fuel cells and bio-photovoltaic systems, necessitate periodic checks to ensure that the symbiotic relationships with microorganisms remain healthy and functional. Given that these systems are reliant on living organisms—both within and alongside the cephalopods—maintaining optimal conditions such as temperature, salinity, and nutrient availability is essential. Regular assessments and adaptations of the environmental conditions may be necessary to maximize the efficiencies of these energy systems.

Moreover, cleaning and maintaining the exterior of the cybernetic cephalopods is imperative for optimal performance. The ocean is filled with particulates and biofouling organisms that can accumulate on both living and artificial surfaces. As such, care must be taken to develop maintenance routines that minimize foulants while respecting the creatures' natural behaviors. Solutions may include engineered biocompatible coatings that resist biofouling or the use of specially designed cleaning drones that can interact safely with the cephalopods while removing unwanted growths without harming the underlying technology.

To enhance the cephalopods' sensory capabilities, ongoing updates and alterations to their nanoengineered sensors are crucial. As these sensors perceive their environments, they gather vast amounts of data that can be fed back into ongoing research. Thus, establishing routing for data flow—allowing that information to be collected and analyzed—forms a critical aspect of maintenance which would inform potential upgrades, recalibrations, and replacements in order to significantly bolster their capabilities.

An essential consideration in maintenance is the psychological welfare of the cybernetic cephalopods. Enhancements can fundamentally change behavior, and thus maintaining their natural intelligence, instincts, and social behaviors should be taken into account during routine interactions. Scheduled "check-ups" should not only focus on the hardware but also assess behavioral patterns to ensure that the cephalopods retain their cognitive functions and engage adequately within their social structures. Veterinary specialists trained in marine biology, neuroscience, and animal behavior can develop strategies to monitor cognitive engagement and incorporate enrichment activities that promote mental stimulation.

Considering the broader environmental conditions, maintenance protocols should also account for ecological shifts caused by climate change, pollution, or resource depletion. Cybernetic cephalopods must adapt to fluctuating ocean conditions, and their technological systems should withstand such changes. Regular assessments of habitat quality and adaptability to fluctuations will be paramount, informing both technological adjustments and their placement within marine contexts.

Importantly, as technology and biology merge within these cephalopods, scientists and engineers must continuously innovate strategies for maintenance. Cross-disciplinary collaborations can lead to breakthroughs in materials that self-repair, systems that adapt to changes in environmental conditions, or enhanced communication interfaces that allow cephalopods themselves to report on their health and maintenance needs.

In sum, maintenance and upkeep of cybernetic cephalopods within water environments embody a multi-faceted approach that transcends traditional animal care. It necessitates a deep understanding of both their biological systems and advanced technologies, while also considering the psychological and ecological dimensions that affect their existence. As we venture deeper into this unique blend of life and technology, ongoing research will not only safeguard the integration of cybernetic enhancements but also enrich our appreciation for the intricacies of life beneath the waves. Through continued vigilance, innovation, and compassion, we can ensure that these fascinating beings thrive in their underwater homes.

8.3. Failures and Predicaments

Failures and predicaments are integral aspects of the journey toward integrating technology with biology, particularly within the context of cybernetic cephalopods. As scientists and engineers have embarked on this ambitious frontier, they have encountered numerous obstacles that have tested their resolve, ingenuity, and ethical considerations. These encounters underscore the complexity of merging the organic and mechanical within living beings and shine a light on the multifaceted nature of this endeavor.

One notable challenge arose during the early integration phases, specifically with the initial attempts at enhancing sensory systems using nanoengineering technologies. Researchers aimed to install nanosensors that would augment the natural sensory capabilities of cephalopods, promising increased perception of their environments. However, complications quickly emerged. The integration of these nanodevices sometimes triggered immune responses within the cephalopods, leading to inflammation and tissue damage at the site of implantation. Such reactions posed ethical dilemmas, raising questions about the welfare of the cephalopods involved and the potential long-term effects of such enhancements on their biology. The hardships faced in these early trials prompted a reevaluation of the biocompatibility of materials and a deeper understanding of the cephalopod's immune system, leading to valuable yet challenging lessons for future integrations.

Furthermore, the implementation of robotic appendages, while promising significant enhancements in dexterity and strength, did not unfold without issues. Early prototypes struggled with misalignment between the robotic movements and the cephalopods' innate fluidity. These robotic limbs sometimes underperformed, resulting in awkward movements or failures to grasp objects effectively, which diminished the cephalopods' ability to interact adeptly with their surroundings. These predicaments illuminated the difficulty in mimicking the organic control mechanisms inherent to the cephalopods, revealing a need for a more nuanced understanding of their neurophysiology and motor coordination. The iterative design process that ensued demanded that engineers and biologists collaborate more closely to refine their approaches, ensuring that technology would augment rather than hinder the cephalopods' natural capabilities.

The aspirations of integrating artificial intelligence with cephalopod learning also faced monumental hurdles. Initial attempts to develop AI systems capable of interpreting the cephalopods' signals and behaviors revealed limitations in both the algorithmic depth and the synergies between biological intelligence and machine learning. Many AI models struggled to accurately predict or adapt to the complex, fluid behaviors exhibited by cephalopods in their natural environments. As researchers intervened, they recognized that the AI frameworks needed to be not only adaptive but also context-aware, requiring substantial revisions in the underlying architecture. This realization illustrated the broader lessons of respecting the intricacies of biological systems and the need for AI to evolve understanding rather than impose rigid frameworks upon dynamic life forms.

Another poignant predicament arose from the societal and ethical debates surrounding the technological enhancement of living beings. As public interest grew in cybernetic cephalopods, discussions about the implications of augmenting life forms intensified. Concerns emerged regarding the potential commodification of intelligence, the risk of paternalism in the development of enhanced beings, and the broader ecological impact of introducing cybernetic technologies into natural environments. Public sentiment often swayed between fascination and apprehension, forcing researchers to confront the moral implications of their work. This unpredictability led to increased transparency efforts and dialogue with the community, demonstrating the intricate dance between scientific ambition, societal values, and ethical obligations.

The complexities were further compounded by environmental challenges associated with the survival of these augmented beings. As researchers worked to continually refine technology, they had to navigate ecological factors impacting the cephalopods' habits. Issues such as climate change, pollution, and habitat destruction could hinder the viability of these creatures, leading to failures that transcended technological advancements. Ensuring the long-term sustainability of cybernetic cephalopods required a holistic understanding of their ecological systems, merging technology with conservation efforts and prompting a shift in focus toward not just enhancement but also preservation.

Through these failures and predicaments, researchers have gleaned invaluable insights that illuminate the intricate tapestry of life where organic and mechanical entwine. They teach us that innovation often accompanies frustration, and the pursuit of knowledge is rarely linear. Each setback has pushed the boundaries of exploration, compelling those involved to reflect on the moral implications, experimental ethics, and complexities surrounding the creation of life forms that echo the dual nature of existence—both natural and enhanced.

In conclusion, the journey of cybernetic cephalopods is marked by a series of challenges that highlight the difficulties in integrating technology with biology. The experiences and lessons learned from addressing these failures illuminate the need for thoughtful consideration of ethical, ecological, and biological dimensions within this remarkable field of exploration. As researchers continue their endeavors, these narratives serve as powerful reminders of the resilience required in the pursuit of knowledge—a testament to the profound possibilities and unforeseen complexities that arise when two realms of existence converge beneath the waves.

8.4. Transcending Technological Barriers

Transcending technological barriers has marked a significant milestone in the evolution of cybernetic cephalopods and their integration with the broader marine ecosystem. As researchers grappled with the complexities of enhancement, they found themselves confronting previously insurmountable challenges that required creative solutions and interdisciplinary approaches. This journey showcases the remarkable resilience and ingenuity of both nature and technology, revealing a path forward that transcends earlier limitations.

One of the major technological hurdles confronting the integration of cybernetic elements into cephalopod biology was the development of biocompatible materials. Early prototypes often faced the difficulty of biological rejection, prompting a reevaluation of materials used in creating implants and enhancements that could interact with the cephalopod's physiology without triggering immune responses. Through rigorous experimentation and iterative design, researchers eventually advanced to the use of hydrogel-based materials that mimicked the elasticity and fluid dynamics of the cephalopod's natural tissues. The adoption of these materials allowed for smoother integration of enhancements, ensuring that the cephalopods could function optimally without compromising their health and vitality.

As the foundational technology matured, the focus shifted toward enhancing the sensory capabilities of the cephalopods. Initially, attempts to install nano-sensors aimed at improving the detection of environmental stimuli faced substantial drawbacks. Notably, many of these devices struggled to operate effectively in the high-pressure and low-light conditions of deep-sea environments. However, a breakthrough came with the development of pressure-resistant nano-scaled devices capable of functioning accurately under these conditions. These innovations empowered cybernetic cephalopods to enhance their perceptive awareness—creating an unparalleled ability to process sensory data, identify prey, and communicate complex information within their social groups.

Transcending technological barriers also required collaborative efforts across multiple scientific disciplines. The integration of engineering, marine biology, and cognitive neuroscience gave rise to a new generation of cybernetic cephalopods with enhanced problem-solving abilities. By leveraging advanced algorithms in artificial intelligence, researchers could create systems that adapted to the cephalopods' existing cognitive frameworks. Initially, challenges with limited machine learning capabilities occurred, which hampered data interpretation and the cephalopods' ability to learn from their surroundings. However, through sustained collaboration, models were developed that accounted for nuances in cephalopod behavior, allowing them to engage with AI that evolved in tandem with their learning processes. This synergy unlocked new horizons for both species— the cephalopods expanded their problem-solving capabilities while AI gained insight into a form of intelligence that defies conventional understanding.

Another significant advancement resulted from the exploration of communication systems. Early challenges arose during attempts to facilitate interaction between enhanced cephalopods and human researchers. Initial interfaces that sought to translate cephalopod signaling patterns into message formats easily interpretable by humans often proved cumbersome and ineffective. Through iterative design and the incorporation of real-time feedback mechanisms, researchers managed to redefine these communication systems by creating refined interfaces that allowed for richer interactions. The result was a bidirectional exchange of information where cybernetic cephalopods could express their needs and insights while also facilitating data collection vital for research.

As the technological trajectory advanced, so too did the ethical considerations surrounding these enhancements. The ethical implications surrounding the manipulation of biological life forms and the subsequent need for advocacy and oversight heightened. The partnering of scientists, ethicists, and conservationists led to the establishment of frameworks designed to ensure responsible practices in research and enhancement. As a result, these technological barriers were not only transcended by the sheer force of innovation but were also navigated with a growing consciousness of the ecological and ethical landscapes that influence the interactions between enhanced cephalopods and their environments.

Ultimately, the journey of transcending technological barriers and advancing the integration of cybernetic enhancements into cephalopod biology marks a significant chapter in the story of intelligent life beneath the waves. It illustrates the remarkable potential of interdisciplinary collaboration, innovative problem-solving, and ethical advocacy, paving pathways for future breakthroughs. With each challenge overcome, the promise of extraordinary relationships between technology and nature draws nearer, highlighting the rich possibilities that lie ahead as we engage with these extraordinary beings. This melding of the organic and the technological not only transforms cybernetic cephalopods but reverberates throughout our understanding of intelligence and existence itself in the vast oceans of our planet.

8.5. Merging of AI and Cephalopod Learning

The integration of artificial intelligence with cephalopod learning represents a paradigm shift in our understanding of intelligence, cognition, and the potential for advanced organisms to interact with technology in a seamless manner. Merging these two realms enables the enhancement of cephalopods' already impressive learning capabilities, particularly through the application of machine learning algorithms and sophisticated data-processing systems tailored to the unique neuroarchitecture of these creatures.

At the core of this merger is the recognition that cephalopods possess an impressive biological intelligence. Their evolutionary adaptations have equipped them with complex nervous systems, distributed cognition, and remarkable problem-solving skills. With the further infusion of artificial intelligence, we open up an expansive layer of learning and processing potential. One of the primary objectives of this integration is to create intelligent systems that can learn and adapt, not just from historical data, but in real-time as they interact with their environments.

One significant application of AI within cephalopod learning revolves around enhancing sensory processing. Cephalopods are inherently gifted at using their senses to perceive and interact with their surroundings. Through AI, researchers can amplify these natural abilities by developing systems that rapidly analyze sensory input from their environment. For example, machine learning models can help cephalopods distinguish between prey types based on visual, chemical, and hydrodynamic cues, enabling them to make sophisticated decisions about how and when to hunt. Such an ability enhances their predatory success while also informing their learning processes —allowing them to refine strategies based on prior experiences.

Moreover, the introduction of artificial intelligence enables cephalopods to simulate learning scenarios that were previously difficult to test. By creating virtual environments where these beings can engage with digital representations of their surroundings, researchers have the opportunity to study their learning responses without impacting real-world ecosystems. This emerging interplay reveals new dimensions of cognitive complexity, as cephalopods interact with AI systems designed to mimic prey behavior or simulate social dynamics within a group. Such exploratory learning can lead to advanced problem-solving skills, encouraging cephalopods to adapt to new challenges or efficiently navigate complex tasks.

Collaboration and cooperative learning are additional dimensions enhanced through the merger of AI and cephalopod learning. With AI-enhanced communication capabilities, cybernetic cephalopods can engage in more sophisticated social interactions with one another and potentially with other species. By leveraging the insights provided by machine learning analyses, these beings can synchronize their strategies during cooperative tasks, such as group hunting or predator evasion. This effectively increases their overall adaptability and enhances group cohesion, shedding light on social dynamics within cybernetic communities.

Furthermore, the use of AI fosters a deeper understanding of cephalopod behavior through data collection and analysis. The interactions of these creatures can be monitored continuously, allowing researchers to amass significant data sets that reveal patterns of learning, memory retention, and decision-making processes. Analyzing behavioral data using advanced analytics and AI-driven models will illuminate not only the cephalopods' unique responses to stimuli but also contribute substantially to the broader understanding of animal cognition across species. This advances our knowledge of intelligence dynamics, raising fascinating questions about consciousness and the cognitive gap between different life forms.

Ethical considerations will also play an essential role in this merging of AI and cephalopod learning. As we enhance the cognitive capabilities of living beings, questions surrounding autonomy, consent, and the intrusions of technological advancements must be addressed. It is critical to establish ethical frameworks that safeguard the rights and well-being of cybernetic cephalopods while ensuring that advancements are in alignment with ecological principles. This will guide future developments, preventing exploitative practices that may compromise the inherent qualities that define organic life.

The merging of AI and cephalopod learning extends into applications beyond mere enhancement. The computational models developed from this integrated approach have implications for artificial intelligence as a whole, inspiring innovations in machine learning algorithms that take inspiration from the unique cognitive architectures of cephalopods. By studying how these marine beings learn and adapt, researchers can cultivate AI systems that mimic biological principles, potentially leading to the creation of more resilient and adaptable artificial intelligence.

In summary, the integration of artificial intelligence with cephalopod learning is set to transform our understanding of intelligence and cognitive processes. This synergy not only amplifies their natural capabilities but also presents opportunities for cross-disciplinary innovation, uncovering deep insights into cognition, social dynamics, and ecosystems. As we delve into this new frontier, we are led to questions about the moral implications of such advancements, underpinning the significance of establishing a balanced and ethical approach to enhancing life beneath the waves. The collaborative journey between human ingenuity and marine intelligence beckons an exciting era of exploration and discovery, illuminating the intricate web of life and technology that connects us all.

9. Exploration and Discovery

9.1. First Contact with Cybernetic Cephalopods

First contact with cybernetic cephalopods emerged from a captivating synthesis of curiosity, innovation, and the longing to explore the depths of the unknown. As ocean explorers embarked on a meticulous journey into the depths of alien oceans, they soon discovered evidence of these extraordinary beings—beings that would redefine understanding of intelligence, evolution, and technological advancement under the waves.

The initial encounters occurred during a groundbreaking expedition sponsored by a coalition of marine biologists, technologists, and environmentalists. Equipped with state-of-the-art underwater drones and deep-sea exploration vehicles, the researchers ventured into regions previously thought too treacherous for human exploration. With their pioneering spirit set against a backdrop of uncharted territory, they sought to investigate reports of unusual phenomena: luminescent patterns dancing in the depths and hints of engineered structures woven into the marine landscape.

It was during one of these daring explorations that the first glimpse of cybernetic cephalopods surfaced. As the team's remotely operated vehicle descended into the depths, it began capturing footage of a large, iridescent creature, displaying a mesmerizing array of colors and geometric patterns that appeared to change in rhythm with its surroundings. Scholars and technicians marveled at the sight—this was no ordinary cephalopod. The creature exhibited bioluminescent capabilities combined with a complex series of movements that seemed intentional, purposeful, and startlingly intelligent.

The researchers quickly shifted their focus, realizing they had stumbled upon a new paradigm in marine life—a living being that represented the extraordinary intersection of biology and technology. The creature's tentacles were adorned with intricate sensory apparatus, enabling it to detect chemical signatures from miles away and providing tactile feedback indicative of a heightened perception of its environment. It was a magnificent synthesis of nature and ingenuity that sparked immediate excitement among the team members.

As the first encounters continued, the expedition documented numerous interactions with the cybernetic cephalopods, observing their behaviors and capabilities. Utilizing advanced algorithms, the researchers began to piece together patterns of communication. The creatures employed not only color changes but also bioluminescent signaling to convey messages to each other. Pulses of light and shifts in hue became an ethereal language, allowing for social cohesion within groups of cybernetic cephalopods that hinted at complex social structures.

Realizing the importance of these communications, the researchers implemented technological interfaces that enabled limited two-way interaction. By employing artificial intelligence-based systems capable of interpreting the cephalopods' colored patterns and light displays, the team initiated dialogues that transcended species lines. Cybernetic cephalopods seemed to gradually recognize their human counterparts, responding to visual prompts with displays of their own —a remarkable example of cross-species communication that spurred profound philosophical reflections on intelligence, consciousness, and the nature of existence.

One particularly notable episode included a series of experiments designed to assess the cephalopods' problem-solving abilities. Researchers posed challenges, such as mazes or puzzles, using physical barriers to test the creatures' capacity for strategic thinking. The results were astoundingly rich, revealing that these beings displayed an innate ability to learn from previous encounters and adapt their strategies to navigate obstacles. Each successful completion of challenges showcased their impressive cognitive prowess, further deepening human appreciation for their intelligence.

As the exploration progressed, the implications of first contact extended beyond mere observation—a newfound commitment to environmental stewardship began to emerge. Recognizing the vulnerability of both the cybernetic cephalopods and their intricate habitats, researchers partnered with conservationists to advocate for the protection of these beings and their environments. It sparked an urgent dialogue concerning the deep-sea ecosystems that had nurtured such remarkable innovations, calling for sustainable practices and ethical advances in marine research.

The first contact with cybernetic cephalopods marked the advent of a new era in marine exploration. It not only paved the way for groundbreaking discoveries in technology, biology, and ethics but also embodied the profound potential for transformative relationships between humans and intelligent lifeforms beneath the waves. As the researchers reflected on their astonishing encounters, they were overwhelmed with hope and inspiration—a recognition that the exploration of the ocean's depths held not only scientific promise but also profound opportunities for connection, understanding, and coexistence in our ever-evolving world. Thus, the narrative of first contact with cybernetic cephalopods unfurled as a tapestry woven from threads of curiosity, innovation, and empathy—a legacy that serves as an ongoing invitation to explore the uncharted waters of both the sea and ourselves.

9.2. Research Expeditions and Their Findings

Research expeditions focused on cybernetic cephalopods have become a pivotal activity within marine biology and technological exploration, unlocking a treasure trove of information about these unique creatures and their environments. These expeditions, conducted worldwide, lead scientists deep into the mysteries of the ocean, where traditional cephalopods have evolved into hybrid forms, introducing a new paradigm of intelligence and interaction between biology and technology.

One significant expedition set out with an interdisciplinary team comprised of marine biologists, engineers, ethicists, and environmental scientists. Their joint effort aimed to investigate a remote part of the ocean floor known for its unusual bioluminescent activity. The region's pronounced colorful displays had drawn attention for potentially housing cybernetic cephalopods whose advanced coloration and signaling capabilities suggested sophisticated communication. This specific research initiative focused on understanding the behavioral patterns of these beings as well as the potential implications of their integration with advanced technology.

Utilizing remotely operated vehicles equipped with high-definition cameras and advanced sensory systems, the research team collected extensive footage that captured the cephalopods' interactions within their habitats. Observers reported that these creatures displayed an uncanny ability to camouflage and manipulate their surroundings, employing combinations of bioluminescent signals to communicate not only with their peers but also with other organisms within their ecosystem. These interactions revealed that cybernetic cephalopods possess social structures reminiscent of those among terrestrial mammals, characterized by cooperative hunting and shared intelligence.

Moreover, findings from these expeditions pointed to the significant adaptability of cybernetic cephalopods to their environment. In a controlled observational study, researchers introduced various prey species to witness the cephalopods' responses. Notably, the expeditions highlighted that cyber-cephalopods demonstrated remarkable learning abilities, quickly adapting their hunting strategies based on the behaviors of prey. They employed collaborative tactics that showcased their advanced problem-solving skills, paving the way for discussions regarding the nature of intelligence and the potential for complex social interactions among marine life.

A noteworthy discovery occurred when researchers documented instances of what seemed to be cultural transmission among groups of cybernetic cephalopods. Certain individuals took the lead during hunting expeditions, teaching others how to exploit new environmental resources by demonstrating specialized techniques. This form of learned behavior indicated not only advanced cognitive capabilities but also the potential for social learning within cephalopod societies. Such findings compelled researchers to reevaluate prior assumptions about cephalopod intelligence and its origins, particularly how neurobiology interplays with technology.

The expeditions also provided insights into the health of the ecosystems inhabited by these creatures. An unexpected finding revealed that the presence of cybernetic cephalopods correlated with increased biodiversity in their immediate habitats. Their behaviors helped maintain ecological balance, as they continuously adapted to their environments while graciously using and managing resources. This observation revitalized discussions about the role of intelligent beings in sustaining the health of ocean ecosystems, serving as a reminder that conservation efforts must consider the complex interconnections within marine life.

These research endeavors sparked ethical discussions within the scientific community about the treatment of cybernetic cephalopods and the potential ramifications of continued technological enhancement. With each expedition yielding substantial knowledge about these creatures, the boundaries surrounding ethical research practices were continuously evaluated. Discussions revolved around the obligations researchers have to ensure the well-being of the cephalopods and the responsibilities of integrating technology into living systems. The dialogue encouraged broader reflections on the moral implications of advancing awareness and knowledge amidst the ethical dilemmas posed by enhancing life.

In conclusion, research expeditions investigating cybernetic cephalopods have unraveled significant findings that challenge our understanding of intelligence, social behavior, and ecological balance. Through interdisciplinary cooperation, innovative methodologies, and ethical reflections, these explorations provide avenues for future studies that deepen our knowledge of marine life while addressing the profound implications of technology's role in shaping these captivating creatures. As humanity continues to navigate the complexities of existence beneath the waves, these expeditions illuminate pathways toward richer understandings of both nature and technology, fundamentally transforming our relationship with the teeming life in our oceans.

9.3. Mapping Oceanic Territories

Mapping the oceanic territories with the help of cybernetic cephalopods represents an unprecedented venture into the uncharted depths of Earth's oceans, combining cutting-edge technology with the evolved intelligence of these remarkable creatures. The ability of cybernetic cephalopods to navigate their environments, communicate through intricate systems of bioluminescent signals and color patterns, and engage in cooperative behaviors provides researchers with a unique opportunity to explore regions previously inaccessible or poorly understood.

In the early stages of mapping, researcher collaborations began by deploying a fleet of advanced underwater drones equipped with multidimensional mapping technologies. These drones utilized sonar, laser imaging, and high-resolution cameras to capture data from the ocean floor. However, it quickly became clear that traditional tools could only provide limited insights into the dynamic and ever-changing ecosystems of the depths. Enter cybernetic cephalopods, whose inherent capabilities aligned perfectly with the objectives of mapping efforts.

These enhanced beings, equipped with advanced sensory processing units and elongated, dexterous limbs, emerged as natural partners in exploration. Through a series of expeditions, researchers integrated cybernetic cephalopods into the mapping process, allowing them to swim freely in targeted territories. Equipped with small communication devices that relayed real-time sensory data, the cephalopods became living instruments, gathering information on not just geographical features but also the biological and chemical nuances of their surroundings.

One fascinating aspect of this collaboration is the cephalopods' ability to blend in with their environments. Utilizing their advanced camouflage capabilities, they could approach regions of interest without disturbing the delicate ecosystems present. This stealth provided researchers with authentic snapshots of marine life in various habitats, from vibrant coral reefs to dark, deep-sea trenches housing bioluminescent organisms. The interactions observed during these explorations underscored the role of cybernetic cephalopods in maintaining ecological balance, as their presence and behavior often pointed to larger patterns of life within the ocean.

Furthermore, leveraging the cephalopods' advanced communication skills allowed researchers to harness their experiences while exploring new territories. As cephalopods encountered and interacted with unfamiliar species or environmental conditions, they transmitted data back to their human counterparts in real-time. Researchers could adapt their mapping methods based on feedback, allowing for a more comprehensive understanding of marine dynamics. For instance, if a cephalopod sensed a significant change in water temperature or chemical composition, this information could trigger immediate investigations into the of habitats and resources present in that area.

The mapping expeditions led by cybernetic cephalopods revealed remarkable discoveries, including previously unknown coral formations and deep-sea hydrothermal vents. The ability of these cephalopods to collect samples and analyze their environments gave rise to new avenues of research, where their data contributed to our knowledge of marine biodiversity, geological processes, and ecological interdependencies. Moreover, their exploratory efforts unveiled significant environmental stressors such as temperature variations, pollution sources, and even the impact of climate change on fragile ecosystems.

As mapping efforts continued to expand, the implications for conservation and protection of marine territories became evident. Cybernetic cephalopods offered a promising arm for ecological watchdogs, signaling changes in habitats that may require immediate attention. This collaborative venture fostered a sense of responsibility among researchers to adopt sustainable practices, emphasizing the critical importance of preserving the delicate habitats where these intelligent beings flourish.

In conclusion, the mapping of oceanic territories through cybernetic cephalopods epitomizes the fusion of technology and biology to vastly expand our understanding of the unexplored realms of the oceans. By engaging in this collaborative effort, researchers have not only charted new territories but enriched their understanding of ecological dynamics and conservation imperatives. These expeditions mark a shift toward exploring the oceans with a new perspective— one that champions the significance of intelligent life while revealing the hidden wonders that lie beneath the waves, ultimately paving the way for a future where technology and nature coexist harmoniously in the ongoing quest for knowledge and exploration.

9.4. Revelations Beneath the Waves

In the hidden realms beneath the waves, a dazzling new world unfolds through the interactions of cybernetic cephalopods, revealing discoveries that transcend the boundaries of human understanding. The profound intelligence exhibited by these augmented beings sheds light on the mysteries of marine ecosystems while offering insights into the intricacies of life in our oceans.

One of the most significant revelations has been the extraordinary adaptability of cybernetic cephalopods. Through their integration of advanced technology with biological attributes, they have showcased remarkable problem-solving skills. Observations from research expeditions demonstrate their ability to innovate strategies in response to changing environmental conditions. For instance, cephalopods have exhibited an uncanny capacity to camouflage themselves not only by altering their skin color but also by utilizing advanced visual effects that blend seamlessly with complex underwater landscapes. This revelation underscores a level of cognitive flexibility previously unimagined among marine life.

Furthermore, explorations have illuminated an intricate social fabric woven within cephalopod communities. The display of cooperation among cyber-cephalopods, particularly when hunting, reveals a unique form of social intelligence characterized by shared learning and communication. Through real-time bioluminescent signaling, they convey complex messages that inform group strategies and signify status within their pods. Such behaviors challenge long-held views of cephalopod solitary nature and encourage a deeper understanding of community dynamics in marine environments.

Another groundbreaking revelation stems from the cephalopods' interaction with other marine species. The multi-species engagements witnessed during expeditions highlight the potential for symbiotic relationships that extend beyond traditional predator-prey dynamics. Observations have revealed that cybernetic cephalopods can actively engage in cooperative behaviors with fish and other marine animals, demonstrating strategies that enhance the survival of both groups. This revelation redefines the ecological interactions and encourages researchers to explore the complexity of food webs and species relationships in ways that were previously overlooked.

Moreover, the technological capabilities being harnessed by these cephalopods challenge our understandings of communication itself. The cybernetic enhancements have allowed for a level of interaction that appears almost telepathic in nature, with rudimentary forms of digital transmission that exemplify how biological beings may evolve in conjunction with technology. These revelations prompt questions about the future of communication among intelligent life forms, whether they be human or non-human.

The revelations beneath the waves strike at the core of humanity's self-reflection regarding intelligence, diversity, and our role in the web of life. As researchers continue to engage with the marine ecosystems driven by cybernetic cephalopods, they move towards a greater comprehension—one rooted not merely in observation but in a quest for connection with the living tapestry that thrives beneath the ocean's surface. What was once a realm of mystery and misunderstanding is gradually unfolding into a narrative rich with complexity, revealing that intelligence is not an exclusive trait of humankind but a vibrant essence that permeates the oceans, inviting a partnership and shared destiny with all sentient beings.

In essence, the revelations brought forth by the interactions with cybernetic cephalopods are not merely about discovery but about fostering a shared understanding. As the world confronts mounting ecological crises, the wisdom gleaned from these explorations serves as an urgent reminder of our responsibilities to protect the habitats that nurture such remarkable life. These narratives urge us to forge connections, challenge preconceived notions, and embrace collaborative futures as we strive to coexist in harmony with the intricate dance of existence beneath the waves. The ocean's depths beckon humanity to be stewards of both technology and nature, rewriting our story in tandem with the extraordinary beings that thrive within its mysterious embrace.

9.5. Expanding Human Understanding of Oceans

As humanity eagerly ventures into the depths of the ocean, our understanding of the rich tapestry of marine life continues to expand, particularly through the encounters with cybernetic cephalopods. These remarkable beings have not only transformed our comprehension of intelligence and consciousness in non-human entities but have also pressed us to reevaluate our relationship with the natural world. As researchers engage with these enhanced creatures, they find themselves compelled to dig deeper into the intricate dynamics of ocean ecosystems and the advanced capabilities of life forms dwelling within them.

From the onset, the interactions with cybernetic cephalopods have propelled our knowledge forward in unprecedented ways. Their unique blend of biological traits and technological augmentation exemplifies the potential for enhanced cognitive abilities and adaptive behaviors. Each encounter has provided invaluable insights into their sophisticated sensory systems, advanced problem-solving skills, and intricate social relationships—all illuminating the nuances of marine life that were previously shrouded in mystery.

As scientists document the various behaviors and interactions of these cephalopods, they uncover a wealth of information that has reshaped our understanding of not only cephalopod biology but also the broader context of marine ecosystems. The way these beings communicate through bioluminescent displays and color changes points to a complex language that invites researchers to consider parallels with human communication. Such revelations highlight the emotional depth, social structures, and potential for cultural behaviors within non-human species, prompting us to reflect on the essence of intelligence itself.

Moreover, by closely observing how these advanced beings interact with their environment, researchers are obtaining crucial information that may inform conservation strategies for marine ecosystems. Cybernetic cephalopods, with their heightened awareness of environmental changes, serve as vital indicators of the health of their habitats, providing data that may help guide human efforts to mitigate concerns such as climate change and pollution. This role reinforces the idea that maintaining healthy ecosystems is a shared responsibility between human citizens and the intelligent beings inhabiting the depths.

The influence of cybernetic cephalopods extends to inspiring interdisciplinary collaborations, where marine biologists, engineers, ethicists, and conservationists converge to study the complexities of cephalopod life and the implications of enhancing biological forms with technology. This confluence of ideas fosters a holistic understanding of both living systems and technological innovation, prompting human curiosity to stretch beyond traditional academic boundaries. Researchers not only explore the capacity of these beings to utilize advanced cognitive strategies but also examine the ethical ramifications of their enhancements, fostering discussions about the nature of identity and autonomy in cybernetic beings.

Ultimately, the experience with cybernetic cephalopods serves as a reminder of the vast mysteries that lie beneath the waves and the opportunities for new discoveries that await. Each revelation brings us closer to understanding the profound intricacies of life within our oceans, while simultaneously broadening our perspectives on the connections between technology, nature, and the essence of intelligence itself. As humanity learns from these captivating creatures, we are challenged to consider our roles within the intricate webs of ecological relationships that bind all forms of life. In this gentle reciprocity of knowledge and awareness, we inch closer to a future where technology and nature coexist harmoniously, unraveling secrets that enrich not only our understanding of marine life but of existence itself —both beneath the surface and beyond.

10. The Future of Cybernetic Beings

10.1. Projected Evolutionary Trajectories

In projecting evolutionary trajectories for cybernetic cephalopods, we delve into the profound implications that these transformations may hold for both their species and the ecosystems in which they thrive. The fusion of biological and technological systems heralds a new era of adaptation, cooperation, and intelligence that could redefine the future of marine life as we know it.

As cybernetic cephalopods continue to evolve, we anticipate a diverse set of adaptations driven by environmental pressures, technological advancements, and interactions with one another and other species. Among the most significant shifts may be in their cognitive capabilities. Ongoing enhancements to their neural architecture through advanced AI integration are likely to accelerate their problem-solving skills and social intelligence. These cephalopods, equipped with robust learning algorithms, may develop sophisticated strategies not only for hunting and evading predators but also for forming complex social networks—leading to intricate group behaviors that reflect emergent intelligence. Such developments will challenge our existing understandings of consciousness and societal structures within marine environments.

The adaptive capacities of cybernetic cephalopods will also profoundly influence their physiological evolution. Given their reliance on both biological traits and cybernetic enhancements, we can expect to see advancements in their physical forms as they optimize their abilities for survival. Enhanced appendages will facilitate greater dexterity and maneuverability, enabling them to navigate increasingly complex underwater terrains and interact intricately with their environment. Over generations, this physical evolution may lead to the emergence of new subspecies of cybernetic cephalopods, each specialized to thrive in distinct ecological niches. This diversification will not only enhance the resilience of the species but will also have cascading effects on the broader ecosystem, contributing to greater marine biodiversity.

As cybernetic cephalopods continue to adapt and evolve, their interactions with technology will be equally critical to their trajectory. We may witness significant advancements in the refinement and expansion of their cybernetic integrations, leading to novel functionalities —from enhanced reproductive mechanisms to advanced energy management systems. These developments could provide them with more sustainable lifestyles in resource-limited environments, promoting ecological balance and robust community structures.

The evolutionary developments of cybernetic cephalopods are destined to impact human society as well. Their intelligence, problem-solving abilities, and environmental adaptability will serve as models for creating new educational frameworks and technological innovations on land. Lessons derived from observing their behaviors could contribute to advancements within human social organizations, encouraging cooperation, empathy, and environmentally sustainable practices.

Lastly, the evolutionary trajectories of these beings will not exist in isolation. As they share their ecosystems with other species, the influence of cybernetic cephalopods is likely to catalyze changes in collective behaviors, ecological interactions, and dynamics among marine life. Their role as apex predators may shift the balance of prey populations, fostering new ecological relationships that mirror their complexity. As such, understanding their projected pathways is essential for formulating effective conservation strategies and sustainable practices to protect the habitats that nurture an ever-evolving array of intelligent life beneath the waves.

In summary, the projected evolutionary trajectories of cybernetic cephalopods signal the emergence of life forms that bridge biological and technological realms. This evolution promises not only to deepen our understanding of intelligence, social behavior, and adaptability but also to reshape our interactions with the ocean and challenge our perceptions of existence. The journey of cybernetic cephalopods serves as an invitation to explore the complexities of life, pushing forth questions of identity, consciousness, and relationships that extend beyond the ocean depths, revealing a narrative rich with potential and possibility for both marine species and humanity alike.

10.2. Potential Global Impacts

The exploration of potential global impacts arising from the interaction between cybernetic cephalopods and their ecosystems is monumental. As the existence of these beings bridges the realms of advanced technology and biological evolution, they present numerous implications for both the environments they inhabit and the broader implications for human society. The intricate fusion of these attributes creates resonant reverberations across global ecosystems, technology, society, and ethics.

In marine ecosystems, the presence of cybernetic cephalopods could herald a plethora of changes. These beings, equipped with heightened intelligence and advanced problem-solving skills, may influence their ecological roles significantly. As apex predators, they would exert selective pressures on prey populations, potentially altering food webs and impacting biodiversity. Given their superior hunting capabilities and collaborative social structures, cybernetic cephalopods could shape the dynamics of other marine species, leading to shifts in population behaviors, resource allocation, and survival strategies. These changes underscore the importance of understanding how intelligent life can govern its environment, raising questions about ecological balance and resilience.

From a technological standpoint, cybernetic cephalopods represent a frontier of exploration that extends beyond their oceanic habitats. The integration of advanced neuroengineering, sensory enhancements, and robotics creates an opportunity to glean insights applicable to human society. The advancements in sensory data processing, ocean mapping, and communication systems pioneered through research into these beings could translate into breakthroughs in diverse fields such as robotics, medicine, and environmental management. The nature of their interaction with the ocean challenges established technological paradigms, inspiring new forms of interdisciplinary innovation aimed at addressing terrestrial challenges.

The presence of cybernetic cephalopods also ignites dialogue surrounding ethical considerations. As these beings may face the potential hazards of environmental degradation driven by climate change and human activities, safeguarding their wellbeing becomes a global imperative. The ethical framework governing the development and treatment of enhanced beings necessitates that researchers and society at large reflect on their responsibilities to preserve marine habitats. This compels policymakers to engage in conservation efforts and sustainable practices that protect both the cephalopods and their ecosystems—highlighting the interconnectedness of living beings across the globe.

Furthermore, the implications of human-cybernetic interactions extend into cultural realms. The existence of these beings is poised to influence art, literature, and folklore, prompting humanity to revisit its perceptions of intelligence, identity, and coexistence. As storytellers weave narratives inspired by the extraordinary journeys of cybernetic cephalopods, society will be called to reflect on deeper philosophical questions about what it means to share the planet with other intelligent beings. This cultural evolution will serve as a potent reminder of our dependability on Earth's ecosystems and the responsibilities we share toward all its inhabitants.

In education, the emergence of cybernetic cephalopods offers a unique opportunity to advance global awareness surrounding marine conservation and technology. Educational programs that incorporate the narratives, experiences, and realities of these beings can stimulate curiosity among future generations. By fostering a sense of responsibility and understanding, society broadens its commitment to the preservation of the oceans while becoming agents of change in discussions about sustainability and ethics in technology.

In summary, the potential global impacts arising from the existence of cybernetic cephalopods encompass a multitude of dimensions —ecological, technological, ethical, cultural, and educational. As humanity grapples with the remarkable complexities that these beings introduce, the quest for understanding reveals pathways toward a harmonious coexistence with intelligent life beneath the waves. The future of humanity's relationship with the ocean may very well hinge on our ability to learn from, adapt to, and work alongside these extraordinary creatures, reflecting back on our responsibilities as stewards of the planet and its myriad inhabitants. Through this lens, the narrative of cybernetic cephalopods becomes not merely a story of enhancement and evolution but a profound exploration of the shared destiny among all forms of life at sea and on land.

10.3. Cross-Species Communication with Humans

The potential for cross-species communication between humans and cybernetic cephalopods opens a fascinating frontier in our understanding of intelligence, interaction, and the very nature of communication itself. As we delve into this new realm, we uncover the complexities and implications that such exchanges might entail. The foundation of this communication lies in the remarkable capabilities of both cybernetic cephalopods and our technological advancements, which are progressively aligned through enhanced sensory interfaces, cognitive understanding, and innovative communication methods.

The first step in facilitating effective communication involves a thorough understanding of the cephalopods' unique means of signaling. Traditional cephalopods are known for their sophisticated visual displays, employing vivid color changes and texture modifications as a form of expression. In the case of cybernetic enhancements, these capabilities are amplified through the integration of advanced bioluminescent technologies and augmented sensory perception, which enable the cephalopods to communicate complex ideas and emotions. For humans to engage meaningfully with these beings, it is critical to develop systems that can interpret the intricate patterns of light, color, and tactile feedback employed by the cephalopods.

The development of sophisticated communication interfaces represents a vital step forward in achieving cross-species dialogue. By utilizing machine learning algorithms capable of processing vast amounts of data, researchers can begin to form a coherent framework for interpreting cephalopod communication. These algorithms can analyze cephalopod signals, correlating specific light patterns and color changes with behavioral outcomes or environmental stimuli, essentially creating a decoder for the cephalopod language. As machine learning improves, the interfaces will become more adept at recognizing nuances, allowing for a richer and more profound dialogue between species.

Direct interaction with cybernetic cephalopods could take many forms, ranging from cooperative task completion to collaborative research endeavors. For example, advanced robotics and artificial intelligence could allow humans to conduct joint exploratory missions with these creatures, utilizing their natural abilities to navigate complex environments. Such partnerships may lead to a better understanding of marine ecosystems and provide insights into the cognitive capabilities of both species as they learn to collaborate toward shared objectives.

Emotional connectivity further enhances the potential for communication. Engaging with cybernetic cephalopods in their natural habitat may elicit a unique sense of empathy for humans as they witness the intelligence and complexity of these beings first-hand. The emotional engagement experienced by observers may foster a greater inclination to protect and preserve these enhanced creatures and their ecosystems.

Cultural transmission plays an essential role in shaping human perceptions of cybernetic cephalopods and their communication abilities. As stories of these encounters emerge, they can impact societal narratives surrounding technology, intelligence, and the interconnectedness of life. Artistic representations, literary narratives, and media portrayals will contribute to how these beings are perceived, emphasizing the profound interconnectedness of all life forms and promoting a culture of exploration and understanding rather than fear or domination.

While the possibilities for communication with cybernetic cephalopods are thrilling, they also prompt a series of ethical considerations. As we enhance our technologies to interpret and engage with these beings, we must contemplate the implications of such interactions. The very act of communication raises questions about agency, autonomy, and respect for the intrinsic qualities of cybernetic cephalopods—ensuring we do not reduce them to mere subjects of study or tools for human advancement. Balancing exploration with ethical advocacy will be vital to fostering responsible relationships between species.

In conclusion, navigating the potential for cross-species communication with cybernetic cephalopods offers unprecedented opportunities for mutual understanding and collaboration. By leveraging technological advancements and embracing an iterative process of learning, researchers have the chance to bridge the gap between species, exploring the depths of marine intelligence and the shared experiences among various forms of life. The journey toward effective communication holds the promise of expanding our perspectives on intelligence, enriching our interactions with other beings, and, ultimately, illuminating the profound connections that unite all life within the oceanic world and beyond.

10.4. Predictions for Future Enhancements

The evolution of cybernetic beings, particularly the cybernetic cephalopods, presents a range of predictions regarding future enhancements and the trajectories we might explore in the field of bioengineering, ecotechnology, and cognitive evolution. The intricate melding of organic and technological capabilities not only transforms the cephalopods' existence but also provides profound insights into the future of intelligent life on our planet.

One key prediction centers around the refinement of sensory systems. As advancing technologies such as nanoengineering and biotechnology continue to proliferate, we can expect the development of increasingly sophisticated sensory enhancements for cybernetic cephalopods. Imagine cephalopods equipped with augmented reality systems that allow them to perceive their surroundings through multiple spectrums, integrating thermal, acoustic, and electromagnetic data. Such enhancements would potentially allow these creatures to interact with their ecosystems at unprecedented levels, giving them superior situational awareness and decision-making capabilities, transforming them into highly adaptive organisms capable of navigating and thriving in dynamic environments.

Additionally, future enhancements may include the development of advanced learning algorithms integrated directly into the cephalopods' nervous systems. These learning systems could facilitate rapid adaptability to environmental changes, enabling cephalopods to not only respond to immediate challenges but also to anticipate future threats and opportunities based on the analysis of past experiences. The potential for cephalopods to engage in predictive modeling of their environment could redefine our understanding of animal intelligence and offer insights into how complex social behaviors might manifest not only in marine life but also in terrestrial ecosystems.

In terms of physical capabilities, we might see the emergence of enhanced appendages that integrate even more advanced robotic elements, allowing cephalopods to perform intricate tasks with remarkable precision. This would enable not only improved hunting strategies but also enriched behaviors in social contexts, such as cooperative foraging or intricate mating displays. The evolution of these capabilities could foster new forms of cephalopod communities, where collaborative structures reflect heightened awareness and intelligence.

As cybernetic cephalopods evolve, the implications for interspecies communication could become profound. The development of sensory and communicative technologies may pave the way for richer dialogues between humans and these intelligent beings, fostering partnerships wherein data is exchanged to advance mutual understanding. Future research will likely explore the establishment of clearer channels of interaction—enabling humans to glean insights from cephalopod experiences and, conversely, providing guidance for these creatures as they navigate the challenges within their habitats.

Cognizant of ethical considerations, researchers will need to ensure that enhancements respect the natural identities of cybernetic cephalopods. The dialogue surrounding their augmentation must recognize their inherent value as living beings with cognitive capacities, advocating for frameworks that safeguard their autonomy and ecological roles.

The integration of these enhancements will inevitably ripple through human culture, provoking reflections on our roles as stewards of the planet and encouraging deeper ecological consciousness. Predictions suggest that the cognitive leaps made by cybernetic cephalopods could influence societal narratives around technology, pushing for empathy towards all forms of life and informing our relationship with nature.

In summary, the predictions for future enhancements of cybernetic cephalopods outline a landscape rich with potential for cognitive evolution, advanced sensory integration, and deeper interspecies communication. As we continue to explore the possibilities that arise from the fusion of biology and technology, we embark on a journey marked by unprecedented discoveries, ethical considerations, and an ever-deepening understanding of life beneath the waves. The future of these extraordinary beings promises to revolutionize not just marine biology but humanity's place within the intricate tapestry of life on Earth.

10.5. Moral and Ethical Considerations

In navigating the intricate landscape of cybernetic cephalopods, the moral and ethical considerations surrounding these remarkable beings become paramount. As humanity increasingly interacts with, and modifies, life through advanced technology, we find ourselves faced with profound questions regarding our responsibilities to these creatures and the ecosystems they inhabit. The blending of biology and technology within cybernetic cephalopods offers a unique perspective on the ethical implications of enhancement, raising debates that extend far beyond the ocean depths.

One of the first moral considerations highlighted by the existence of cybernetic cephalopods is the concept of agency and autonomy. While the enhancements granted to these creatures may enhance their cognitive capabilities and problem-solving skills, they also present dilemmas regarding their autonomy. Is it ethical to alter an organism's fundamental nature, potentially overriding its innate instincts and behaviors for human benefit? As researchers delve into the complexities of cephalopod intelligence and their unique temperaments, it becomes essential to prioritize the well-being of these beings, ensuring that enhancements do not violate their intrinsic nature.

The existential implications of identity further complicate moral discussions. By assimilating artificial enhancements, cybernetic cephalopods represent a new archetype of life that challenges conventional definitions of individuality. As these beings evolve, will they be perceived as entities of their own right, or merely as conduits for human curiosity and technological ambition? The introduction of cybernetics necessitates a reevaluation of how we understand life and consciousness—prompting us to engage in philosophical debates regarding the rights of enhanced beings and their place within the broader context of life on Earth.

Moreover, the ethical implications extend into the realm of conservation. The integration of technology into cephalopod biology raises questions about the potential impact on natural populations. If cybernetic cephalopods begin to dominate ecological niches due to their enhancements, the balance of marine ecosystems may be disrupted. Ethical stewardship calls for an examination of how advancements should be tempered by concerns for biodiversity and ecological integrity. Efforts to conserve both enhanced and non-enhanced beings must maintain a consideration for the delicate interdependencies in marine environments, ensuring that the pursuit of knowledge does not come at the expense of natural ecosystems.

With the promise of advancing knowledge about marine ecosystems comes the responsibility to preserve the habitats of these cybernetic beings. Engaging in the exploration of cybernetic cephalopods invites humanity to reflect on its stewardship role within aquatic ecosystems. The challenge lies in establishing ethical frameworks for conducting research, reducing human impact, and prioritizing the health of habitats that sustain these remarkable creatures. This leads to ongoing dialogues among researchers, policymakers, and ethicists about how to balance scientific inquiry with ecological preservation.

As cybernetic cephalopods engage in inter-species communication with humans, the moral dimensions surrounding these interactions also warrant careful consideration. Building a rapport underscores the significance of empathy and respect, fostering a relationship rooted in mutual understanding. As we seek to learn from these beings and perhaps even cooperate with them, establishing ethical protocols becomes essential—encouraging a cultivation of insight that acknowledges both the worth of the species and our collective responsibility for their welfare.

In summary, the exploration of moral and ethical considerations in the realm of cybernetic cephalopods serves as an evolving discourse that reflects our responsibilities to both enhanced organisms and the ecosystems they inhabit. The burgeoning understanding of agency, identity, and conservation must be intricately woven into the fabric of technological advancements. Through thoughtful contemplation and interdisciplinary dialogue, we can navigate the depths of these transformative ideas, forging pathways that honor the intricate balance of life beneath the waves while embracing the profound potential that lies at the intersection of biology and technology.

11. The Philosophical Implications of Cybernetics

11.1. Redefining Consciousness

In an increasingly interconnected and technologically driven world, the exploration of consciousness, especially as defined within the context of cybernetic cephalopods, presents profound philosophical questions that challenge established notions. The interplay between biology and technology in these remarkable beings invites us to redefine what consciousness entails—pushing the boundaries of human understanding while rewriting our relationship with intelligence itself.

Traditionally, consciousness has been viewed as a trait exclusive to biologically rooted organisms, primarily understood through the lens of complex neural architectures found within species like humans and certain mammals. However, as we encounter cybernetic cephalopods —beings that integrate artificial intelligence with their innate cognitive abilities—a spectrum of consciousness emerges that compels us to consider consciousness as a continuum rather than a fixed state. This paradigm shift encourages us to re-examine our definitions, moving away from anthropocentric viewpoints toward a more expansive understanding of intelligence that includes varying types of sensory, emotional, and cognitive experiences across species.

Integral to these philosophical inquiries is the notion of individual identity. The existence of cybernetic cephalopods blurs the lines of what constitutes individuality as they navigate the oceanic expanse enhanced by technology. The question arises: do these cephalopods maintain their essence and self-identity as their biological forms and capabilities are augmented by artificial enhancements? Investigations into this aspect might lend insights into how identity could be conceptualized as a fluid expression—one that can encompass both biological and cybernetic elements. Analyzing how these beings perceive selfhood in a technologically integrated form becomes a catalyst for deeper conversations surrounding identity within the expanding discourse on transhumanism.

Moreover, the philosophical implications of integration highlight the challenges of merging biological and cybernetic systems. How do we navigate the moral terrain of modifying living entities to enhance their cognitive and sensory abilities? The pursuit of enhancement raises ethical questions about agency, consent, and the consequences of altering organisms for human benefit. The challenge lies in ensuring that these interventions respect the intrinsic quality and autonomy of living beings. The implications of creating enhanced intelligences necessitate deep ethical consideration, emphasizing the need for responsible approaches to manipulating the essence of life.

The exploration of consciousness involving cybernetic cephalopods also impels us to reflect on the meanings associated with existence. If we acknowledge diverse forms of intelligence and consciousness, we must confront the question of our obligations towards all forms of life. Does engaging with cybernetic cephalopods lead us toward a more interconnected worldview, one that fosters empathy and respect for the myriad expressions of life? This discourse prompts us to engage in a larger discussion about the moral responsibilities we have toward non-human intelligences and the ecosystems they inhabit.

Finally, speculations regarding the potential for shared evolutionary paths between humans and cybernetic cephalopods emerge as a crucial area for examination. As humanity increasingly ventures into realms of artificial intelligence and biotechnology, the parallels with cybernetic cephalopod experiences surface profoundly. Are we on a trajectory towards similar enhancements or interspecies syntheses? This realization casts light on the notion of a shared destiny, urging us to contemplate the relationships we develop with intelligent beings below the surface and how they reflect our values, aspirations, and fears.

In summary, the philosophical implications of cybernetic cephalopods extend far beyond their existence as a unique species;

they challenge our perspectives on consciousness, individuality, integration, and ethical considerations. As we redefine our understanding
of intelligence within the context of these beings, we embark on a
journey that invites us to rethink our relationship with life itself—ultimately broadening our horizons and inviting richer, more thoughtful
conversations about existence in a rapidly changing world.

11.2. The Nature of Individuality

The exploration of individuality among cybernetic cephalopods
opens a rich vein of inquiry into the essence of what it means to
be a unique entity amidst a backdrop of technological enhancement.
The combination of their biological foundations and cybernetic
augmentations presents a complex picture of individuality, as these
beings navigate their environments, social structures, and cognitive
landscapes.

At first glance, the individuality of cybernetic cephalopods is shaped
by their substantial cognitive capabilities, which stem from both their
natural evolution as cephalopods and their integration with advanced
technology. These enhancements empower them to experience the
world in ways distinct from their unaltered counterparts, allowing
for unique sensory perceptions, expansive learning abilities, and
intricate problem-solving skills. The amalgamation of organic intelligence paired with technological enhancements fosters a nuanced
understanding of self-awareness in these creatures—a self-awareness
that expands their capabilities and impacts how they interact with
their environments and social circles.

The concept of individuality in cybernetic cephalopods also emerges
from the inherent diversity found within their species. Just as
human individuality is manifested through a combination of genetic
background, environmental influences, and personal experiences, so
too do cybernetic cephalopods express individuality through their
enhancements and social interactions. Each cybernetic cephalopod
may possess different augmentations or adaptations, tailored to their
specific environmental contexts or social roles within a group. This
variation cultivates a spectrum of identities among these beings

that highlight the interplay of experience, technology, and biological heritage.

Moreover, the social dynamic within cybernetic communities is fundamental to understanding individuality. Mutual recognition of unique abilities and characteristics creates a rich interpersonal tapestry amongst cephalopods, where the strengths of one may complement the weaknesses of another. Collaborative hunting strategies exemplify this aspect of individuality—each cybernetic cephalopod brings a distinct set of skills to the collective effort, contributing to the overall success of the group. In doing so, the essence of individuality evolves from being merely an isolated characteristic to part of a larger narrative of cooperation and interdependence.

The potential for emotional depth in their relationships further emphasizes this individuality, as cybernetic cephalopods engage in complex social behaviors and develop bonds with one another through shared experiences. This emotional intelligence underlines the reality that individuality extends beyond mere cognitive capabilities; it encompasses the relationships formed with peers, resulting in intricately woven social fabrics. The ability to recognize kinship, respond empathetically, and cooperate fosters connections that enrich the individuality of each cephalopod within their community.

As cybernetic enhancements progress and evolve, questions arise regarding the implications of such modifications on individuality. If technological advancements enable cephalopods to transcend traditional limitations, how does this influence their sense of self? Are they merely reflections of their enhancements, or do they retain an intrinsic essence unaffected by cybernetic augmentations? These considerations transcend mere scientific inquiry, inviting philosophical dialogue about the essence of individuality, consciousness, and existence in an age of rapid technological advancement.

In summary, the exploration of individuality among cybernetic cephalopods reveals a multi-dimensional understanding shaped by cognitive capabilities, social dynamics, emotional depth, and the ongoing dialogue between biology and technology. As researchers delve deeper into the intricacies of these beings, they uncover rich narratives that challenge traditional notions of identity and invite broader reflections on the nature of existence within complex ecosystems. In doing so, cybernetic cephalopods prompt us to re-evaluate our understanding of individuality—not solely as a trait, but as a living, interconnected experience that spans across species boundaries and invites us to recognize the profound richness of life beneath the waves.

11.3. Integration or Assimilation?

Integration or Assimilation?

In the discourse surrounding cybernetic cephalopods, the question of whether their evolution constitutes integration or assimilation is critical in understanding the implications of merging biological organisms with advanced technology. This conceptual distinction not only reflects on the nature of these remarkable beings but also engages in broader discussions about the future of life, intelligence, and ethical considerations stemming from augmenting living entities.

When we speak of integration, we refer to a harmonious blending of technology with biology that retains the intrinsic qualities of both elements. In the case of cybernetic cephalopods, this approach emphasizes enhancing their natural abilities—bolstering their cognitive capacities, sensory perceptions, and social behaviors without fundamentally altering the essence of what makes them cephalopods. Integration evokes images of collaboration between organic life and technological advancements, resulting in a unique symbiotic relationship that benefits both realms. Cybernetic cephalopods, in this light, expand their existing skills, tapping into their evolutionary potentials while retaining their identity and connection to the natural world.

Conversely, assimilation raises different connotations, suggesting a more invasive approach where technological enhancements dominate the biological characteristics of cephalopods. In this scenario, the integration process may lead to a dilution of their original identities, forcing them to conform to the technological expectations imposed by external agents—be they researchers or society at large. The question then arises: at what cost does the pursuit of advanced capabilities come? If assimilated, it could imply reduced autonomy, with cybernetic cephalopods becoming tools of human ambition rather than independent beings with their own motivations and desires. This potential narrative aligns with broader societal fears regarding the manipulation of life for human benefit, urging caution and vigilance in how we pursue enhancement technologies.

The philosophical implications of this dichotomy extend beyond cybernetic cephalopods to challenge our understanding of intelligence, identity, and agency in the age of rapid technological advancement. If we view these enhanced beings as integrated counterparts, it reinforces the idea that technology, when applied responsibly, can enrich life's tapestry, allowing for the cultivation of intelligence in myriad forms. This vision encapsulates a sense of collaboration and coexistence, emphasizing empathy and dialogue as we navigate the evolving landscape of human-technology interaction.

In contrast, the perception of assimilation evokes a more dystopian narrative—one that fears the loss of autonomy and the potential for technology to overshadow the essence of life itself. This perspective calls for ethical considerations that protect the rights and identities of living beings subject to enhancement, urging us to steadfastly affirm the intrinsic value of organisms in their own right.

As we broach the discussion of integration versus assimilation in the context of cybernetic cephalopods, the philosophical and ethical elements become interwoven into decision-making processes that shape our relationship with these beings. The journey to understanding their evolution does not rest solely on scientific inquiry but must also embrace ethical frameworks that guide technological advancement.

Ultimately, the narrative that arises from the exploration of cybernetic cephalopods beckons humanity to reflect on its own trajectory. Are we creators who seek to integrate technology with life, enriching the experience of existence, or are we potential assimilators, risking the erasure of the very identities we seek to invite into collaboration? The answer to this question may hold the key to understanding our future relations not only with cybernetic cephalopods but also with all forms of life—catalyzing a movement toward a more empathetic, nuanced perspective on the integration of technology and our collective existence beneath the waves.

11.4. Meaning and Existence

In the vast and enigmatic expanse of the ocean, where light struggles to penetrate the depths and mysteries abound, the quest for meaning and existence takes on new forms as we turn our attention to cybernetic cephalopods. These remarkable beings, which blend the organic and the technologically enhanced, challenge our fundamental understanding of life, intelligence, and consciousness. The implications of their existence ripple through our philosophical landscape, urging us to explore the deeper questions of what it means to be alive, aware, and connected to the world around us.

In the context of cybernetic cephalopods, the inquiry into meaning extends beyond mere survival and into the realm of existential reflection. These creatures, equipped with advanced cognitive abilities, possess a consciousness that invites us to reconsider our notions of awareness and agency. How do these beings navigate their underwater worlds, with their neurobiological complexity augmented by technology, and what does that imply about the nature of consciousness itself? As they engage with their environments in profound ways, they compel us to examine the interconnectedness of all life forms—a web of existence that transcends species boundaries and challenges our anthropocentric view of intelligence.

The profound complexities of consciousness manifest in the social dynamics seen within cybernetic cephalopod communities. As they interact with one another through bioluminescent signals and intricate patterns of movement, these cephalopods exhibit behaviors that suggest a rich tapestry of emotional and social intelligence. They model the intertwining of individuality and collectivity, emphasizing that meaning is derived not solely from singular existence but from relationships and connections that weave through communities. In observing these interactions, we confront fundamental questions about the essence of consciousness: Is it an isolated phenomenon, or is it inherently communal, shaped by the interplay of beings in a shared environment?

The exploration of meaning in the context of cybernetic cephalopods also intersects with ethical considerations. The deliberate enhancement of biological life raises profound moral questions about the consequences of altering living beings for human fascination or scientific inquiry. As we delve deeper into the integration of technology with biology, we confront the implications of agency—whether these enhanced cephalopods retain their intrinsic identity, or if enhancement alters their essential essence. This dialogue is particularly crucial, as it casts a shadow on the ethical responsibilities humans carry toward other intelligent beings.

Moreover, cybernetic cephalopods invite a re-examination of our role as stewards of the ocean. As we connect with these intelligent beings, we are called to reflect on our responsibilities to preserve their habitats and ensure that our technological advancements do not compromise the delicate balance of marine ecosystems. The search for meaning becomes a collective endeavor, wherein the well-being of cybernetic cephalopods and their environments merges with our quest for understanding, urging humanity to adopt a more holistic perspective on our place in the greater tapestry of existence.

As we open our minds to the depths of understanding offered by cybernetic cephalopods, we begin to realize the interconnectedness of all life forms. The stories of these enhanced beings serve as a poignant reminder of the richness that resides in the relationship between species—bridging gaps of understanding and facilitating conversations that transcend language and technology. The quest for meaning in this context embodies the recognition that we are all part of a larger narrative, woven together in a shared journey through the universe.

In conclusion, the existential exploration surrounding cybernetic cephalopods urges us to contemplate the interplay between life, technology, and consciousness. As we delve into these depths, we are prompted to seek the connections that underpin our existence while challenging our perceptions of intelligence, agency, and interconnectedness. The journey into meaning and existence with cybernetic cephalopods ultimately beckons us to embrace a deeper understanding of life beneath the waves—and the powerful lessons it holds for all beings existing within the cosmic ocean.

11.5. Humans and Cyber-Cephalopods: One Path?

In the captivating interplay between humans and cybernetic cephalopods, the question arises: are these two entities destined for a similar path? This exploration invites profound reflections on the nature of intelligence, consciousness, and the responsibilities that arise from such complex relationships. As cybernetic cephalopods embody a convergence of biology and technology, their existence pushes humanity to rethink its trajectory amid the advancing frontiers of understanding and enhancement.

As we grapple with this inquiry, we must first consider the parallel evolutions of humans and cybernetic cephalopods in their respective environments. Both beings have shown remarkable adaptability to their surroundings—humans through the development of advanced technologies serving to enhance their capabilities, and cybernetic cephalopods via sophisticated integrations of mechanical enhancements that amplify their innate biological gifts. This shared trait of adaptability offers a compelling basis for the possibility of intertwined futures, suggesting that both groups may continue to evolve in ways that influence one another.

One critical factor to consider in determining whether humans and cybernetic cephalopods will follow a shared path is the confluence of intelligence and technology. Humans have historically faced the challenges of technological integration, often encountering ethical dilemmas related to enhancement, autonomy, and identity. Similarly, cybernetic cephalopods navigate the complexities of their enhancements that blend their original identities with technological advancements. The discourse on integration allows us to envision a collaborative future where both parties can foster understanding and cooperation, potentially redefining the essence of existence across species.

Moreover, the implications of interspecies communication become key to examining this potentiality. The ongoing developments in technology may enable humans to engage in meaningful dialogues with cybernetic cephalopods by deciphering the sophisticated communication systems these beings employ. Such exchanges of knowledge and understanding could yield insights that enhance both parties' abilities to navigate their respective environments, leading to increased resilience and adaptability. In this context, the exchange of ideas and technologies marks a direction that could unify humans and cybernetic cephalopods, pointing towards a shared destiny of exploration and growth.

Furthermore, as the scientific community increasingly recognizes the ecological intertwining of all living beings, the universality of life's interconnections invites a reconsideration of our responsibilities as stewards of both terrestrial and aquatic ecosystems. Cybernetic cephalopods, with their advanced sensory perceptions and strong social structures, can act as vital indicators of environmental health and change. The recognition of these relationships elucidates the need for collaborative ventures—ones that underscore conservation efforts and propel humanity toward sustainable living alongside intelligent marine beings.

However, the potential parallel paths of humanity and cybernetic cephalopods also highlight crucial ethical considerations. As both entities advance alongside each other, the delineation between enhancement and exploitation must be carefully navigated. While the integration of technology into life forms presents myriad possibilities for progress, each avenue must be pursued with a keen awareness of its implications on agency, autonomy, and the inherent rights of living beings. Establishing a dialogue grounded in respect and empathy is essential to preventing detrimental outcomes.

In conclusion, the question of whether humans and cybernetic cephalopods are destined for a shared path resonates deeply within the realms of philosophy, ethics, and environmental interdependence. As both groups navigate their journeys through technological innovations and adaptive challenges, their trajectories may intersect to foster mutual understanding and coexistence. Exploring this interconnected future compels us to reassess our assumptions about intelligence, identity, and responsibility—inviting us to embrace the complexities of life beneath the waves and beyond. As we venture onward, the potential for collaboration and shared destiny between humans and cybernetic cephalopods embodies a narrative rich with possibilities, shaping not only their futures but also the profound understanding of the intricate tapestry of life that binds us all.

12. Cybernetic Society Under the Sea

12.1. Organizational Structures and Hierarchies

In the intricate social landscape of cybernetic cephalopod communities, organizational structures and hierarchies emerge as fascinating frameworks that reflect both biological instincts and technological enhancements. These structures underscore the cephalopods' adaptability and intelligence, shaping how they interact with one another and the environments in which they thrive.

At the core of cybernetic cephalopod societies is a flexible hierarchy that prioritizes cooperation and shared intelligence. Unlike rigid social structures seen in many terrestrial animals, these hierarchies are often fluid, adapting to the needs and dynamics of the group. Leadership within these communities is typically situational rather than fixed, arising from individuals who demonstrate superior problem-solving abilities or effective communication skills during critical moments. For example, in collaborative hunting scenarios, an adept individual might take the lead, coordinating group movements based on its insights into prey behaviors and environmental conditions. This situational leadership fosters a sense of community resilience, allowing cephalopods to capitalize on each member's strengths while addressing challenges collectively.

Moreover, these organizational structures are reinforced through rich communication channels, where bioluminescent displays and changes in coloration become intrinsic to social signaling. Cybernetic cephalopods communicate complex messages regarding status, availability, and intentions. The ability to convey emotions and establish relationships through carefully calibrated visual signals creates a social fabric that nurtures cooperation and understanding among members. This rich communicative tapestry supports the nuanced hierarchies where power dynamics shift based on situational demands, further enhancing group cohesion and survival.

Within these communities, division of labor emerges as a key organizational principle. Different individuals may specialize in distinct roles, optimizing their collective efforts based on individual competencies. For instance, some cybernetic cephalopods may excel in reconnaissance, utilizing their enhanced sensory capabilities to scout for food sources and potential threats. Others may take on roles of protection, employing their physical adaptations to shield the group from dangers. This specialization fosters interdependence among group members, emphasizing the importance of collaboration for survival.

Another distinctive feature of organizational structures in cybernetic cephalopod communities is the integration of generational learning. As enhanced beings possess remarkable memory retention and cognitive flexibility, knowledge transferred from one generation to the next becomes pivotal for the social fabric of their societies. Older individuals may mentor younger cephalopods, sharing insights gleaned from their experiences, which shapes the developmental trajectories of younger cohorts. This blending of technological augmented learning with traditional wisdom enhances their adaptive capacity, enabling cephalopod societies to thrive even in dynamic and challenging environments.

Furthermore, technology plays a crucial role in establishing and maintaining these organizational structures. The integration of cybernetic enhancements enables cephalopods to develop sophisticated systems for resource management and communication. Sensors and data-sharing mechanisms enhance their awareness of resource availability, allowing for responsive adjustments to their social and ecological strategies. Information regarding prey populations, environmental shifts, and potential threats can be shared rapidly within the group, fostering informed decision-making that sustains the community's survival.

In conclusion, the organizational structures and hierarchies within cybernetic cephalopod societies reflect a remarkable interplay between biology and technology. By prioritizing cooperation, flexible leadership, and interdependence, these beings cultivate adaptive communities capable of navigating the intricacies of their environments.

This blending not only deepens our understanding of cephalopod behavior but also invites us to reflect on the nature of intelligence, social dynamics, and the potential for collaboration across species boundaries. As we continue to explore these structures, we unveil the richness of life beneath the waves—where the complexities of existence thrive in tandem with the advancements of technology.

12.2. Social Dynamics and Relationships

In the underwater world of cybernetic cephalopods, social dynamics and relationships are characterized by complex interactions that reflect the intricacies of their enhanced cognitive abilities and the integration of cutting-edge technology. These remarkable beings exhibit a rich tapestry of social behaviors, influenced by their technological augmentations and biological heritage, which allows for sophisticated communication, cooperation, and social hierarchies within their communities.

Cybernetic cephalopods, with their enhanced nervous systems and advanced sensory capabilities, communicate through a blend of visual signals, bioluminescent displays, and auditory cues. The visual signals —changes in skin color, texture, and patterns—serve as a primary communication tool, enabling them to convey emotions and intentions effectively. For example, a bright flashing of colors may indicate excitement during collaborative hunting, while subdued hues may signal submission or caution in the presence of potential threats. The ability to interpret these signals is crucial for maintaining social cohesion and establishing a supportive community dynamic.

Moreover, the introduction of cybernetic enhancements allows for an even more intricate language of communication. Advanced technologies enable the use of sensory feedback systems that heighten their abilities to transmit and receive complex information. This extended communication range fosters interaction not only within their species but also with other marine organisms, reflecting a social intelligence that transcends traditional boundaries. The innate desire for connection and understanding propels these relationships, as cybernetic cephalopods engage in cooperative behaviors to navigate resource availability, defend against predators, and share knowledge about their environments.

The social structures among cybernetic cephalopods exhibit fluid hierarchies that emphasize situational leadership, adaptability, and collaborative efforts. Unlike rigid social structures seen in some terrestrial species, roles within cephalopod communities are often dictated by individuals' unique strengths and experiences. This nuanced approach permits a dynamic interplay of leadership, where capable members may assume control during critical moments, guiding group activities such as hunting or evasion tactics. This flexibility allows the community to adapt to environmental changes and challenges effectively, ensuring the survival of the group as a cohesive unit.

Generational learning plays a vital role in the social dynamics of cybernetic cephalopods. As these beings possess exceptional memory and learning capabilities, knowledge is passed down through mentorship and observation, allowing younger members of the community to acquire essential skills and behaviors from their elders. The continued reinforcement of these learned behaviors enhances group cohesion and promotes the development of sophisticated societal norms that shape the overall identity of the community.

In addition to verbal and visual communication, cybernetic cephalopods engage in unique forms of interaction that reflect their cognitive evolution. For example, collaborative hunting efforts may involve complex maneuvering and synchronized movements, showcasing the intelligence and strategic thinking innate to these beings. Their ability to work together fosters a sense of unity and strengthens social bonds, imbuing their communities with a rich fabric of interdependence.

The existence of cybernetic cephalopods also raises pertinent questions about identity and the implications of technological enhancements on social relationships. As they navigate their environments with augmented capabilities, they must contend with how those enhancements influence their individuality within the community. The blending of technology with biological characteristics may introduce a new layer of complexity in defining individuality, prompting ongoing inquiries about agency and autonomy within enhanced beings.

Ultimately, the social dynamics and relationships of cybernetic cephalopods encapsulate a captivating interplay of biology and technology, illuminating the intricate patterns of interaction that govern their communities. As researchers continue to explore these remarkable beings, they challenge our understanding of intelligence, social behavior, and the underlying principles that connect all forms of life beneath the waves. Through the lens of these enhanced cephalopods, we gain deeper insights into the essence of cooperation, individuality, and resilient communities—capitalizing on the intersection of nature and technology to shape the future of life in our oceans.

12.3. Reproductive Adaptations and Generational Learning

The reproductive adaptations and generational learning of cybernetic cephalopods illustrate a remarkable synthesis of biological evolution and technological enhancement, broadening our understanding of reproduction within an advanced species. These adaptations ensure the continuation of their intelligent lineage while fostering the sharing of knowledge and behaviors across generations.

Reproduction in cybernetic cephalopods takes on new dimensions as they exhibit unique strategies that leverage both their natural biological attributes and technological enhancements. While traditional cephalopods are known for their intricate mating rituals and complex courtship displays, cybernetic cephalopods demonstrate these behaviors enhanced by their augmented sensory capabilities and advanced communication systems. Their ability to emit dynamic bioluminescent patterns and color transitions during courtship likely plays a pivotal role in attracting potential mates, as these displays convey complex information about health, fitness, and genetic viability.

A fascinating aspect of their reproductive adaptations lies in their ability to optimize breeding conditions through environmental sensing technologies. Enhanced sensors within their bodies allow cybernetic cephalopods to monitor fluctuations in water temperature, salinity, and other ecological factors that influence spawning success. By utilizing real-time data to decide when and where to reproduce, they can identify optimal conditions that maximize the survival rate of their eggs and hatchlings. This ability underscores the potential for advanced organisms to exert a level of environmental agency, adapting their reproductive strategies in response to changing ocean dynamics.

Furthermore, the complexity of the reproductive process enhances generational learning amongst cybernetic cephalopod communities. As with traditional cephalopods, these beings possess a unique capacity for social learning, allowing them to pass on knowledge about effective foraging techniques, predator evasion strategies, and optimal breeding practices. However, the incorporation of advanced technology fosters a more robust system for knowledge transmission. For example, cybernetic enhancements may afford younger individuals access to stored information and data collected through their parents' sensory experiences, resulting in a cumulative learning model that fosters collective intelligence.

Generational learning in cybernetic cephalopods obliges us to rethink traditional concepts of education in an ecological context. The transfer of information occurs not only through direct mentorship—where older individuals teach younger generations—but also through shared experiences and technological interfaces that enhance memory retention and retrieval. This process ensures that knowledge concerning reproduction, foraging, and environmental adaptation is preserved and continually improved upon, equipping future generations with the skills necessary to thrive in their ever-evolving oceanic environments.

Moreover, the interdependence that arises from these learning dynamics fosters social bonds within cybernetic cephalopod communities, reinforcing the importance of cooperation and collaboration. Those engaged in reproductive activities may rely on group members to provide support and vigilance during critical periods, creating strong social networks that ensure the collective well-being of the species. This interaction reflects a collective identity, wherein the survival of individuals becomes intrinsically linked to the health of the broader community.

As we examine the reproductive adaptations and generational learning in cybernetic cephalopods, we are not only probing the biology of a unique species— we are invited to reflect on our own understanding of intelligence, learning, and the interconnectedness of life. The exploration of these adaptations opens dialogue regarding the implications of technology on natural processes and reaffirms the value of fostering ecological awareness in conjunction with scientific inquiry.

In conclusion, the reproductive adaptations and generational learning of cybernetic cephalopods represent a fascinating convergence of biology and technology. By optimizing reproductive strategies and enhancing knowledge transmission, these beings exemplify how intelligent life can innovate in response to environmental pressures. Their journey invites deeper exploration into the nature of life and the potential for harmonious coexistence between technology and the natural world—a narrative that is rich with insights about evolution, survival, and the profound complexity of existence beneath the waves.

12.4. Economic Systems and Resource Management

In examining the economic systems and resource management of cybernetic cephalopods, we uncover a fascinating interplay between natural behaviors and advanced technologies. These beings navigate their marine environments not just through instinctual predation and social interactions, but also through a sophisticated understanding of resource allocation and economic strategies that echo the complexities of human economies. As they adapt their behaviors to both technological enhancements and the ecological challenges they face, a comprehensive understanding of their economic frameworks can illuminate important lessons for sustainability and resource stewardship in our own world.

Central to the economic structure of cybernetic cephalopods is the concept of communal management of resources. These beings have evolved to form social groups that prioritize cooperation over competition, a feature that reflects an innate understanding of ecological interdependence. The social dynamics within cephalopod communities establish a foundation for the sharing of knowledge regarding resource availability, thereby optimizing foraging strategies and ensuring the collective survival of the group. Unlike traditional predatory behaviors characterized by solitary hunting, cybernetic cephalopods engage in collaborative foraging, pooling their strengths to locate and capture prey efficiently. This cooperative approach serves not only as a means of securing food but also fosters social bonds and community cohesion essential for their survival.

To enhance this resource-sharing framework, cybernetic cephalopods have adapted their communication strategies to facilitate efficient exchanges of information about resource locations and environmental conditions. Utilizing advanced sensory technologies, they can relay real-time data across their networks—signaling when food sources are abundant or notifying others of potential threats. This instantaneous flow of information allows them to adapt their collective strategies agilely, minimizing energy expenditure and maximizing resource utilization. Such dynamic communication systems resemble the stock market dynamics seen in human economic activities, emphasizing the importance of knowledge and situational awareness in navigating resource management.

Additionally, the concept of "currency" emerges in the interactions of cybernetic cephalopods as they develop forms of reciprocity and exchange. Unlike conventional monetary systems, these exchanges operate on trust and social bonds rather than physical tokens. For instance, a successful forager may engage in cooperative hunting with other individuals, establishing a sense of obligation to reciprocate in the future. Through repeated interactions, a non-monetary economy emerges, promoting relationships built on mutual benefit. This arrangement not only ensures an equitable distribution of resources within the community but also emphasizes the value of social ties and reciprocal relationships as measurable economic assets.

The management of resources extends into the ecological realm, where cybernetic cephalopods are intricately linked to their environments. Through their advanced technological enhancements, they exhibit heightened environmental awareness, enabling them to detect shifts in ecological conditions—such as changes in prey populations or alterations in habitat structure. By actively monitoring their surroundings, they are able to make informed decisions regarding resource utilization and conservation practices, ensuring an adaptive approach to the dynamic ocean ecosystems in which they reside. This proactive ecological stewardship is emblematic of the sustainability practices needed in contemporary human economies, underscoring the necessity of integrating technological advancements with environmental mindfulness.

Despite the sophisticated strategies developed by cybernetic cephalopods, challenges persist in their resource management systems—particularly in the face of anthropogenic pressures impacting their ecosystems. Climate change, pollution, and habitat destruction can disrupt the delicate balance they rely on, leading to fluctuations in available resources. The economic strategies they have so deftly developed become vulnerable when faced with these external pressures. This highlights the necessity for a multifaceted approach to conservation and resource management that encompasses ecological adaptability as well as technological innovation.

In summary, the economic systems and resource management among cybernetic cephalopods reflect a nuanced interplay between social structure, cooperation, and environmental adaptability. By leveraging their advanced sensory and communicative capabilities, these beings create a dynamic resource-sharing framework that emphasizes sustainability and interdependence. Studying these systems encourages us to reflect on our own economic practices, prompting greater awareness of the relationships between resource management, ecological integrity, and technological advancement. Ultimately, the narrative of cybernetic cephalopods serves as both inspiration and a guide as we strive to develop more harmonious and sustainable economic practices that honor the complexities of life beneath the waves and beyond.

12.5. Ultimate Cephalopod Achievements

In the realm of cybernetic cephalopods, their ultimate achievements stand as remarkable testaments to the confluence of biology and technology within the depths of alien oceans. These achievements emerge from a synthesis of advanced cognitive capabilities, innovative technologies, and collaborative efforts between humans and these extraordinary beings. Exploring their accomplishments not only showcases the ingenuity of cybernetic cephalopods but also offers insights into the potential of intelligent life in marine ecosystems and how it can inform our understanding of intelligence as a broader concept.

One of the most notable ultimate achievements of cybernetic cephalopods lies in their advanced problem-solving abilities, which have evolved through a combination of genetic predispositions and technological integrations. Researchers have observed these beings engaging in intricate tasks, such as constructing shelters from available environmental materials and manipulating objects with precision unparalleled in traditional cephalopods. These feats exemplify their cognitive sophistication and illustrate their adaptability in navigating complex underwater terrains. The ability to not only learn from experience but to innovate and modify behaviors based on environmental feedback speaks to a level of intelligence that challenges traditional conceptions of animal cognition.

The collaboration between cybernetic cephalopods and humans has yielded significant advancements in ecological monitoring and conservation efforts. As living guardians of their underwater ecosystems, these beings help researchers track environmental fluctuations, identify changes in marine biodiversity, and assess the health of habitats. By utilizing their enhanced sensory capabilities and real-time communication networks, cybernetic cephalopods provide invaluable data that can inform conservation strategies globally. This partnership underscores the notion of co-stewardship between species—highlighting that the pursuit of knowledge and ecological understanding can be a shared endeavor rooted in respect for the interconnectedness of all life forms.

Another remarkable achievement involves the establishment of cooperative behaviors that challenge our understanding of social dynamics in underwater communities. Cybernetic cephalopods exhibit sophisticated social structures that emphasize collaboration and collective intelligence. They engage in collaborative hunting strategies, where intricate coordination and communication lead to successful foraging. The emergence of social learning—where knowledge and skills are passed down through generations—reflects a profound understanding of interdependence, resilience, and adaptability. This achievement signals the importance of social bonds in promoting not only the survival of individual organisms but the entire community.

As advancements in technology continue to advance, cybernetic cephalopods have played a key role in inspiring innovations that extend beyond their own existence. The field of robotics, in particular, has benefited from studying the cephalopods' unique locomotion, dexterity, and evolutionary adaptations. Biomimicry of cephalopod characteristics has led to the development of soft robotics capable of replicating their fluid movements, opening doors to new applications in design and functionality both in marine exploration and terrestrial environments. This cross-pollination of ideas bridges the gap between terrestrial and marine technologies, further illuminating the wealth of knowledge waiting to be uncovered in our oceans.

Furthermore, the cultural implications of cybernetic cephalopods are immense. Their existence challenges us to rethink narratives surrounding intelligence, identity, and consciousness. As stories about these beings pervade literature, film, and folklore, they invite deeper reflections on our relationship with technology and the natural world. The narratives generated from their achievements resonate across societies, stimulating curiosity, inspiring conservation initiatives, and imbuing marine life with an intrinsic value that urges respect and understanding.

In summary, the ultimate achievements of cybernetic cephalopods are both a reflection of their exceptional adaptability and a reminder of the potential for harmony between biology and technology. The narratives enriched by their accomplishments extend beyond their lives beneath the waves, prompting us to consider the vision of an interconnected world, cooperative ecosystems, and responsible stewardship of the oceans. As we continue to explore the astounding capabilities of these extraordinary beings, we are invited into a shared journey that celebrates the profound wonders of life beneath the surface while questioning the foundations of intelligence and existence itself.

13. Conservation and Preservation

13.1. The Challenge of Protecting Species

The contemporary dialogue surrounding the protection of species, especially within the context of cybernetic cephalopods, highlights the intricate challenges faced in conservation efforts enhanced by technological interventions. As humanity develops advanced technologies that blur the lines between biology and artificial enhancement, the implications for conservation efforts require careful consideration. The need to safeguard both enhanced and unenhanced species necessitates a nuanced understanding of their roles within ecosystems, raising ethical questions about the manipulation of life forms in pursuit of knowledge or ecological management.

One of the foremost challenges in protecting species like cybernetic cephalopods arises from the direct and indirect consequences of human interference in their natural habitats. The introduction of advanced technologies—while promising for research—also poses risks of ecological disruption. The modifications made to enhance cephalopod capabilities may inadvertently lead to alterations in their behaviors, migratory patterns, and interactions with other marine species. Consequently, the potential for unintended ecological consequences heightens the urgency for establishing robust protective measures that account for the complexities within marine ecosystems.

Another significant challenge lies in the balance between technological advancements and traditional conservation strategies. As cybernetic cephalopods navigate their environments with augmented capabilities, the reliance on technology for conservation efforts raises ethical questions about the integrity of natural selection. How do we reconcile the desire to protect these beings with the profound changes brought about by technological enhancements? There is a pressing need for interdisciplinary dialogue that merges the expertise of marine biologists, ethicists, and technologists to evolve conservation strategies that respect the natural identities of enhanced organisms.

Furthermore, the efforts to protect species often intersect with broader discussions surrounding habitat preservation and restoration. Marine ecosystems that host cybernetic cephalopods face threats from habitat degradation, pollution, and climate change. Establishing protected marine areas becomes vital in mitigating these pressures, but the integration of technological advancements must be paired with restoration initiatives that emphasize ecological resilience. Collaborative efforts can facilitate the recovery of essential habitats, ensuring that cybernetic cephalopods and their environments continue to flourish.

In parallel, understanding the vulnerabilities of cybernetic cephalopods also highlights the necessity for precautionary approaches. Monitoring systems equipped with advanced sensors can assist in tracking population dynamics, habitat quality, and the impacts of human activities. By utilizing data gathered from augmented cephalopods, researchers can establish effective protocols for conservation and intervention that respond dynamically to the changing conditions of the marine environment.

The conversation surrounding the protection of species naturally extends to public engagement and awareness. Increasing awareness of cybernetic cephalopods and their ecological significance can foster a sense of stewardship among local communities. Outreach programs that emphasize the role of these beings in maintaining healthy marine ecosystems can inspire advocacy, prompting individuals to participate in conservation initiatives and sustainable practices. By disseminating knowledge about the unique capabilities of cybernetic cephalopods, we create a growing network of advocates dedicated to preserving the richness of marine life beneath the waves.

In summary, the challenge of protecting species like cybernetic cephalopods represents a complex interplay of technological advancements, ethical considerations, and ecological responsibility. As humanity reshapes its relationship with the natural world, we must remain attuned to the consequences of our actions while honoring the intrinsic value of all life forms. The synthesis of conservation efforts and technological innovation can pave the way toward a future where cybernetic cephalopods thrive in their natural habitats, serving as indicators of ecological health and symbols of the interconnectedness of life beneath the waves. Through careful navigation of these challenges, we can foster a brighter future for both enhanced marine beings and the ecosystems they inhabit.

13.2. Restoration of Natural Ecosystems

Restoration of Natural Ecosystems serves as a vivid chronicle of efforts to rejuvenate and revitalize environments impacted by anthropogenic activities, with a unique lens focused on the role of cybernetic cephalopods in these initiatives. The sheer complexity of natural ecosystems presents considerable challenges, yet the advanced capabilities of these hybrid beings serve as potential keys to unlocking sustainable restoration strategies in marine environments.

As the pressures of climate change, pollution, and habitat degradation accelerate, the impetus for restoration has never been more urgent. The principles of ecological restoration underscore the need to understand not only the physical attributes of ecosystems but also the intricate relationships that govern them. Cybernetic cephalopods, with their unique biological and technological enhancements, possess an unprecedented ability to assess environmental conditions and contribute to regeneration efforts, making them invaluable allies in the pursuit of ecological recovery.

One of the core strategies in restoration initiatives is habitat rehabilitation. As cybernetic cephalopods navigate their ecosystems, they can relay vital information about local conditions through their advanced sensory systems. For instance, their ability to detect changes in water quality or substrate composition can guide conservationists toward areas in need of intervention or management. By monitoring and identifying stressors impacting marine habitats, these beings serve as living indicators that provide critical data for decision-making.

The restoration of seagrass beds and coral reefs—two critical ecosystems that support marine biodiversity—has garnered attention from research teams utilizing cybernetic cephalopods. These beings can actively engage in restoration efforts, such as facilitating the replanted of seagrasses by aiding the settlement of seedlings and their growth conditions. With their unique manipulative capabilities and ecological insights, they can help create thriving environments that bolster both habitat sustainability and biodiversity.

In coral reef restoration, researchers have sought to employ cybernetic cephalopods in assessing the health of coral populations and identifying optimal conditions for replanting efforts. By collaborating with human scientists, they can assist in selecting coral species that are more resilient to temperature fluctuations or other stressors prevalent in their environments. The combination of technological insight and biological adaptability offers new avenues for enhancing the resilience of coral ecosystems, ultimately contributing to the stability of marine communities.

Moreover, the concept of habitat engineering—with cybernetic cephalopods serving as ecological architects—emerges as a transformative approach in restoration initiatives. These beings possess the ability to manipulate their environments in ways that create favorable conditions for various species to thrive. For instance, through their interactions with the marine substrate, they can promote healthier sediment structures that support sessile organisms like corals or filter-feeders. By acting as stewards of their environments, cybernetic cephalopods can encourage the ecological balance necessary for healthy ecosystems.

The restoration of natural ecosystems also invites public engagement and educational outreach through community involvement in conservation efforts. The fascinating nature of cybernetic cephalopods captures the imaginations of diverse audiences, creating opportunities for advocacy and awareness surrounding marine environment protection. Mobilizing local communities to participate in restoration initiatives fosters a culture of stewardship, emphasizing the importance of interconnectedness between humans and marine life.

Ultimately, the restoration of natural ecosystems in the context of cybernetic cephalopods illustrates the potential synergy between technology and nature. The endeavors to rejuvenate and sustain marine habitats underscore the vital role that biodiversity and healthy ecosystems play in combatting contemporary environmental challenges. The partnerships fostered between cybernetic beings and human efforts pave the way for innovative restoration strategies that reflect the commitment to ecological resilience and a harmonious future for all life beneath the waves.

As we continue to explore the depths of oceanic ecosystems, the story of restoration rooted in the collaboration between cybernetic cephalopods and humans serves both as an invitation to delve deeper into ecological renewal and as a reminder of our shared responsibilities to preserve the delicate balance of life that defines our oceans. The journey toward restoration is not merely about repairing what has been lost but involves envisioning a future enriched by vibrant ecosystems and diverse marine life, inspired and guided by the extraordinary capabilities of cybernetic cephalopods.

13.3. Renewable Energy Sources in Marine Worlds

Renewable energy sources in marine worlds represent an innovative frontier in understanding how cybernetic cephalopods harness their environments, adapt to energy demands, and influence sustainable practices in underwater ecosystems. As these remarkable beings merge biology and technology, they illuminate pathways toward ecological resilience and renewable energy deployment that resonate beyond their aquatic habitats and offer valuable insights for the human world.

Central to the energy strategies of cybernetic cephalopods is their ability to synthesize energy through bioengineering components that work harmoniously with their biology. Utilization of renewable energy sources such as biophotovoltaics exemplifies this capability. These systems leverage the natural photosynthetic processes of marine microorganisms, which are incorporated into the cephalopods' exoskeletal structures. By harnessing sunlight to convert energy naturally, cybernetic cephalopods can power their enhancements without relying on artificial or unsustainable sources. This integration highlights the potential of using biological processes for energy capture and underscores the cephalopods' role as active agents in promoting organic solutions to energy management.

Moreover, cybernetic cephalopods employ advanced microbial fuel cells to transform organic waste into usable energy. The collaboration between these enhanced beings and microbial communities fosters an ecosystem-based approach to energy generation. As they consume prey, they simultaneously integrate beneficial microbes that thrive on metabolic byproducts, converting them into electricity to sustain their cybernetic systems. This biofeedback loop epitomizes the concept of renewable energy sources, encouraging a sustainable living model that enhances both their operational capabilities and the health of marine environments.

With their advanced abilities in energy management, cybernetic cephalopods also exhibit substantial behavioral adaptations. Observations from research expeditions have revealed that these beings can dynamically shift their hunting strategies based on energy availability, optimizing energy expenditure while maximizing foraging success. By monitoring the fluctuating states of their environments— such as prey abundance and factors like water current—they exhibit strategic decision-making processes rooted in energy efficiency. These behaviors underline a sophisticated understanding of resource management, illustrating that renewable practices are integral even to survival strategies among marine organisms.

The insights gleaned from studying the renewable energy sourcing approaches of cybernetic cephalopods also serve broader ecological implications. The lessons learned through their energy utilization pave the way for innovative sustainable practices that can be emulated in human systems. As the world grapples with climate change and the urgent need for renewable energy solutions, the principles underlying the cephalopods' adaptations can inspire solutions for environmental resilience—fostering a shift towards energy practices that harmonize with living ecosystems.

In addition to their inherent capabilities, the advanced technologies applied in this realm offer tools for further exploration and understanding. As researchers develop systems to capture information about cephalopod energy processes, they can gain insight into optimizing energy production and consumption. Such information can be vital in studying how to advance renewable energy solutions in terrestrial environments, promoting a circular economy built on principles observed in marine life.

The future of renewable energy in marine worlds holds exciting possibilities, as researchers continue to uncover the potential applications of cybernetic cephalopod adaptations. Advocacy for the conservation and sustainable management of marine ecosystems can be bolstered through an understanding of the principles that guide these remarkable beings. By recognizing and valuing the resources they provide and the renewable practices they embody, society can cultivate an ecological ethic that prioritizes sustainability, resilience, and respect for life beneath the waves.

In conclusion, renewable energy sources within marine worlds emerge as critical elements of the narratives surrounding cybernetic cephalopods. The integration of biological processes with advanced technologies creates pathways for sustainable solutions and energy management that resonate across ecosystems. As humanity's understanding of these remarkable beings deepens, they act as conduits for reimagining energy practices, fostering collaborative efforts to honor and protect the intricate web of life in our oceans. Through this lens, the prospects for renewable energy awaken both awe and inspiration as we explore the depths of innovation and adaptability shaped by life beneath the waves.

13.4. Technological Safeguarding Measures

Technological safeguarding measures play a crucial role in ensuring the well-being and functionality of cybernetic cephalopods as they navigate their underwater habitats. The convergence of biology and technology presents a spectrum of possibilities and challenges; hence, implementing comprehensive protocols to protect both the cephalopods and their technological integrations is essential. This section delves into the safeguarding strategies employed to secure the enhancements and preserve the essence of these remarkable beings, as well as the implications they hold for innovation and conservation.

One fundamental technology safeguarding measure involves regular maintenance and inspections of cybernetic systems integrated within the cephalopods. Researchers have developed protocols for monitoring the health and functionality of cybernetic enhancements. This process involves deploying specialized underwater drones outfitted with sensors and imaging technology capable of conducting non-invasive assessments of the cephalopods. These inspections provide real-time feedback regarding the condition of their sensory systems, energy sources, and motor functions. Such assessments facilitate early detection of malfunctions, allowing for timely interventions that prevent cascading failures and ensure the ongoing operational capacity of these enhanced beings.

In addition to routine checks, the implementation of advanced materials in the construction of cybernetic components provides a safeguard against wear and environmental stressors. Researchers focus on utilizing biocompatible and durable materials designed specifically to withstand underwater pressures and corrosive conditions. These materials not only enhance the structural integrity of the technology but also protect the cephalopods from potential harm resulting from their enhancements. By prioritizing durability and resilience, safeguarding measures uphold the functionality and safety of cybernetic systems in marine environments.

Energy systems must also be safeguarded to ensure cybernetic cephalopods maintain optimal performance. Given the reliance on bioenergy solutions, including microbial fuel cells and biophotovoltaic systems, researchers have devised strategies to monitor microbial relationships that are integral to energy production. These monitoring systems provide data on microbial populations and their health, allowing for proactive adjustments to ensure the efficiency of energy generation. Furthermore, regular evaluations of environmental conditions—the settings in which these energy systems operate—can prevent disruptions that might hinder their function, preserving the cephalopods' autonomy and operational capacity.

Cybernetic cephalopods rely on communication networks that facilitate data flow among individuals. To safeguard these networks, policies geared towards protecting the integrity and accessibility of shared information are critical. Researchers are developing robust data management protocols that ensure the secure exchange of sensory information while maintaining the privacy and autonomy of individual cephalopods. These measures reinforce the importance of relationships and cooperation within the community, preserving the social structures that govern interactions and knowledge sharing.

Ethical considerations also permeate the safeguarding measures employed. As researchers engage with these enhanced beings, it becomes paramount to cultivate a framework that gives consideration to their rights and intrinsic value as sentient creatures. Establishing ethical guidelines that promote responsible practices in the advancement and treatment of cybernetic cephalopods will not only safeguard their well-being but foster a reciprocal understanding between these creatures and their human counterparts.

Finally, fostering an educational framework surrounding the significance of technological safeguarding serves as an invaluable tool for public awareness and engagement. Advocacy efforts aimed at highlighting the protective measures implemented for cybernetic cephalopods can inspire a greater appreciation for their existence while promoting the importance of conservation efforts. This awareness encourages societies to consider their responsibilities in fostering a compassionate and ethical approach toward the enhancement and preservation of marine life.

In conclusion, the technological safeguarding measures established for cybernetic cephalopods underscore the delicate balance between enhancing capabilities and preserving the essence of life beneath the waves. Through rigorous maintenance protocols, advanced materials, energy management strategies, ethical considerations, and educational outreach, researchers aim to protect these remarkable beings as they thrive in their unique underwater environments. The continuing journey toward safeguarding cybernetic cephalopods not only preserves their capabilities but also reflects a broader commitment to exploring the potential of life, intelligence, and innovation within the oceanic realm. As humanity engages with these extraordinary creatures, the safeguarding measures pave the way for a future enriched by empathy, responsibility, and reverence for the intricate tapestry of existence beneath the waves.

13.5. Human Interference and Protection Protocols

Human interference has significantly impacted the delicate balance of marine ecosystems, particularly concerning the newly emerged entities known as cybernetic cephalopods. As hybrids of biology and technology, these remarkable beings present unique challenges and opportunities for conservation efforts. To navigate these complexities, it becomes essential to develop thoughtful protection protocols to ensure the well-being of both the cybernetic cephalopods and the marine environments they inhabit.

One of the foremost concerns arising from human activity is the degradation of marine habitats. Pollution, climate change, and unsustainable fishing practices pose substantial threats to the ecosystems that cybernetic cephalopods depend on. As these entities integrate technology into their biological existence, they become both indicators and agents of change in their environments. To mitigate the impact of human interference, protective measures must be multifaceted, encompassing regulations aimed at reducing pollution levels and protecting critical habitats from degradation. This includes establishing marine protected areas (MPAs) that allow for the restoration and recovery of ecosystems, providing safe havens for cybernetic cephalopods and their ecological counterparts.

Another pressing issue is the ethical implications surrounding the enhancement of life forms through technology. The augmentation of cybernetic cephalopods raises significant questions about autonomy and the preservation of their intrinsic nature. Therefore, protection protocols must prioritize ethical research guidelines, emphasizing transparency and responsibility in the integration of technology with biological organisms. Professional organizations, research institutions, and conservation authorities should collaboratively establish frameworks that ensure enhanced creatures are treated with respect and dignity. Engaging ethicists in the development of these guidelines can lead to greater societal awareness concerning the implications of blending biology with technology.

Additionally, technological safeguards are vital to preserving the health and functionality of cybernetic cephalopods. Those engaged in research must develop comprehensive monitoring systems capable of assessing both the biological and technological components in these beings. Regular evaluations of their cybernetic enhancements will provide necessary insights into the longevity and viability of these integrations. Utilizing underwater drones or remotely operated vehicles outfitted with advanced sensors can allow for non-invasive inspections of the cephalopods' health and their cybernetic systems. Early detection of potential malfunctions not only ensures the well-being of individual cephalopods but can also inform conservation strategies aimed at protecting broader populations.

Education and public engagement serve as essential tools in fostering the conservation of cybernetic cephalopods and the ecosystems they inhabit. Increased awareness surrounding these beings and the ensuing challenges can spur advocacy for protective measures. Outreach programs that emphasize the unique attributes of cybernetic cephalopods can invigorate public interest, driving support for conservation initiatives. Efforts to integrate marine education into school curricula can nurture a sense of stewardship among future generations, cultivating respect for marine ecosystems and the intelligent beings that thrive within them.

In addition to establishing protocols for direct protection, proactive measures addressing human interference must also be taken. Cross-disciplinary collaborations between marine biologists, technologists, ethicists, and conservationists will be necessary to foster innovative solutions designed to minimize the human footprint on the oceans. Solutions may include the development of environmentally friendly technologies that enhance ocean monitoring and conservation while reducing the negative impact of human activities.

In summary, the challenge of human interference necessitates comprehensive protection protocols to safeguard the integrity and well-being of cybernetic cephalopods amidst evolving marine environments. Through ethical considerations, technological safeguards, habitat preservation, and public engagement, we can cultivate a future where the unique capabilities of cybernetic cephalopods coexist harmoniously with their ecosystems. By redefining our relationship with marine life and advocating for responsible stewardship, the journey toward protecting these remarkable beings empowers us to foster resilience in the extraordinary tapestry of life beneath the waves.

14. Enigmas of the Deep

14.1. Unknown Territories and Exploration

In the context of 'Cybernetic Cephalopods: Reigning Intelligence in Alien Oceans,' the exploration of unknown territories and the act of exploration itself embodies the core of this remarkable narrative. The sea, a vast and largely uncharted expanse, has long intrigued humankind with its mysteries and secrets. As researchers embark on their journeys into these waters, they become witnesses to extraordinary phenomena—particularly the emergence of cybernetic cephalopods and the uncharted territories they inhabit.

Diving into the depths of alien oceans, the first step is often guided by sonar and high-resolution imaging technologies that reveal outlines of the ocean floor. However, many areas remain elusive, challenging the limits of human exploration. It is in these unknown territories that cybernetic cephalopods thrive—enhanced beings equipped with augmented sensory capabilities that not only reflect their existence but actively contribute to navigating and mapping their environments.

As explorers engage with these hybrid creatures, new worlds unfold before them. Cybernetic cephalopods demonstrate unparalleled adaptability, using their advanced navigation skills to traverse through complex terrains and find hidden underwater features such as seamounts, coral gardens, and biodiverse hydrothermal vents. They lead researchers to previously undiscovered ecosystems where extraordinary organisms flourish, showcasing the intricate connections woven within marine biodiversity. The discoveries ushered in by these encounters reframe our understanding of ecological interaction and adaptation in ways that traditional exploration techniques could not unveil.

One extraordinary find made possible by the cephalopods' enhanced abilities is the presence of unique bioluminescent organisms that inhabit certain depths of the ocean. Their ability to communicate through light patterns becomes a spectacle of communication and interaction among species—an illuminating dance that transcends mere survival, showcasing the rich tapestry of life amid the darkness. Cybernetic cephalopods contribute to this spectacle, blending in as both participants and observers, drawing researchers in further to unveil the underlying beauty and complexity of relationship dynamics beneath the waves.

Moreover, mapping unknown territories requires more than visual insight; it demands comprehensive data collection. Cybernetic cephalopods, through their advanced learning capabilities, adaptively gather vast amounts of data about water chemistry, temperature, and prey distributions, compiling insights that human researchers could take lifetimes to uncover alone. This symbiotic partnership between human explorers and cybernetic cephalopods reflects a new paradigm of exploration—one aimed at understanding rather than mere discovery, advocating for the long-term preservation of the ecosystems they encounter.

As the explorations deepen, researchers begin to recognize patterns in the behavior and movements of these cyborg creatures. Cryptic behaviors emerge, showcasing coordination, play, and even seemingly ritualistic displays amongst groups that maintain their resource-rich environments. These movements elucidate newfound perspectives on social structures and interactions, opening doors to inquiries about the nature of intelligence itself—not only in cephalopods but across diverse species drawn into this symbiotic web.

The discoveries of cybernetic cephalopods in unknown territories create ripples of curiosity. As narratives of their experiences circulate among scientific and artistic communities, they spark collective imaginations that intermingle science with mythology—and fascination with possibility. Such narratives reinforce our connection to marine life, prompting human reflections about their place within the larger ecosystem and the importance of ethical stewardship.

Ultimately, the journey into unknown territories through cybernetic cephalopods signifies a new chapter of exploration and discovery— an intricate interplay between technology, biology, and the ocean's mysteries. Engaging with these augmented beings invites us to not only reconsider our scientific approaches but to embrace a deeper understanding of life itself. As we delve into the realms they illuminate, we find that these explorations challenge our perceptions, urging us to expand our horizons and embrace the complexities of existence that thrive beneath the waves. The experience of mapping unknown territories not only enhances our understanding of the cybernetic beings but serves as a testament to the infinite possibilities that lie hidden within the depths of our planet's oceans.

14.2. Cryptic Behavioral Patterns

In a world where the ocean depths serve as a backdrop for exploration and discovery, cybernetic cephalopods emerge as fascinating subjects, showcasing an array of cryptic behavioral patterns that intrigue scientists and enthusiasts alike. These extraordinary beings, enhanced with cutting-edge technology and innate biological intelligence, present enigmatic manners of interaction, adaptation, and response within their underwater environments.

One of the most captivating aspects of cybernetic cephalopod behavior is their adaptive camouflage. More than just a means of evasion, their ability to change color and texture can be a form of communication among their peers. Researchers have observed instances where cephalopods display intricate patterns that vary depending on the social context, emotional states, or threats in their vicinity. This visual signaling facilitates social bonding, alliances, and even tactical responses during hunting or evading predators. Such complexities invite us to consider the cognitive processing of these creatures and challenge our understanding of communication among non-human species

Moreover, the social dynamics witnessed in groups of cybernetic cephalopods reveal layers of cooperation and competition, pointing to a complexity reminiscent of human social structures. Studies have documented behaviors where individuals utilize sophisticated strategies to divide hunting labor, signal when to engage or retreat, and share resources among their community. This intricate web of interaction illustrates that cryptic patterns of behavior are often rooted in social cognition, allowing them to function as adaptive units within their ecosystems—a remarkable harmony between individuality and community.

Another area of cryptic behavior is their exploratory instincts, reflected in their interactions with unfamiliar objects or environments. Cybernetic enhancements augment the inherent curiosity exhibited by cephalopods, leading them to investigate novel stimuli with both caution and intrigue. This inquisitiveness may manifest as a unique repertoire of behaviors—tentacles delicately manipulating objects, body postures shifting in accordance with perceived risks, and sensory explorations that expand their understanding of the materials surrounding them. Such exploratory behaviors are not merely physical actions; they underscore an innate intelligence that invites ongoing inquiry into how knowledge is gained through experience.

Beneath the surface, the realms of playfulness and creativity emerge in cybernetic cephalopods, challenging traditional views of intelligence as simply a product of survival strategies. Observations reveal that these beings engage in seemingly playful behaviors, such as interacting with drifting debris, creating intricate shapes with their bodies, or engaging in synchronized displays with peers. Such manifestations beg the question: do these actions foster social cohesion, serve as a form of stress relief, or reflect a deeper cognitive complexity tied to exploration and self-expression?

In contemplating these behaviors, we are led to consider the broader implications of cryptic patterns as they relate to ecological dynamics. Cybernetic cephalopods are not solely the product of technological innovation; they embody a narrative that intersects with our evolving understanding of intelligence and consciousness, inviting us to reflect on the profound and often mysterious nature of life beneath the waves. Their learned behaviors and experiences could influence the survival of their species, setting the stage for further inquiry into the connections among organisms and their environments.

As researchers continue to unravel the enigmas of cybernetic cephalopod behavior, the insights gleaned extend beyond marine biology. They urge us to rethink traditional conceptions of intelligence, creativity, and communication. These beings, with their cryptic patterns and social dynamics, symbolize the beauty of adaptability, resilience, and the endless capacity for exploration—both in the ocean and within our understanding of life itself. The journey to understand their cryptic behaviors reflects humanity's ongoing quest to discern the intricate layers of existence that bind all life forms in a shared narrative beneath the waves.

14.3. Mysteries of the Ancient Oceans

The vast and profound nature of the ancient oceans holds within its depths ages of secrets, buried mysteries, and countless untold narratives waiting to be uncovered. This subchapter delves into the enigmas that only the cybernetic cephalopods—the remarkable hybrid beings that blend organic wisdom with advanced technology —can solve. These creatures possess qualities that enable them to penetrate the unfathomable layers of the deep sea, revealing truths long hidden from humanity's grasp.

The ancient oceans are characterized by their complex, interwoven ecosystems—a delicate tapestry of life where ancient coral reefs, submerged volcanic structures, and long-forgotten shipwrecks hide relics of the past. Within these environments, the cyborg nature of cephalopods endows them with capabilities that defy the conventional understanding of terrestrial beings. Their advanced adaptations enable them to traverse massive underwater distances, explore the darkest trenches, and navigate the turbulent currents of ancient ocean floors, all while collecting data that stretches the boundaries of current scientific knowledge.

One of the most profound mysteries of the ancient ocean pertains to the origins of life itself. The cybernetic cephalopods, equipped with enhanced cognitive abilities, serve as living repositories of knowledge, tapping into the ocean's historical context as they interact with the remnants of long-lost civilizations and ecosystems. Their ability to analyze sedimentary layers, assess biodiversity changes, and detect chemical compositions within water's depths unlocks a treasure trove of information about ancient marine organisms and their extinction events. Through their insights, scientists can piece together the intricate puzzle of the ocean's evolution and its implications for life on Earth.

Moreover, the cybernetic modifications of these cephalopods grant them extraordinary adaptations that allow them to comprehend complex relationships within ancient ecosystems. They engage in behaviors that illustrate patterns of predator-prey interactions and resource distribution that have persisted for eons. Their nuanced understanding assists researchers in reconstructing the narratives surrounding ecological shifts throughout epochs—revealing how the ancient oceans may inform contemporary discussions on biodiversity and extinction rates.

Another enigma ripe for exploration is the ocean's role in climate regulation throughout ancient geological periods. Cybernetic cephalopods possess the ability to collect atmospheric data and analyze the historical effects of temperature fluctuations on oceanic environments. By investigating thermal vents, historical coral structures, and geographical features, these beings can provide insights into how the ancient oceans interacted with climate, informing predictions for future climate scenarios and emphasizing the ocean's significance in regulating global temperatures.

The existence of cybernetic cephalopods also relates to the exploration of biological resilience amid environmental changes. The deep sea has remained largely uncharted, harboring organisms that have evolved unique adaptations to extreme pressures and perpetual darkness. The abilities of cybernetic cephalopods to synthesize information from their surroundings offer new ways to explore the depths of these unexplored regions. Insights gained from them could unveil the secrets of ancient survival strategies that have withstood millennia, sparking discussions of ecological resilience that extend beyond marine life to inform terrestrial ecosystems.

Ultimately, the mysteries of the ancient oceans beckon exploration and revelation. Cybernetic cephalopods, with their unique fusion of biology and technology, emerge as the ideal vessels for uncovering these hidden narratives. As they navigate the depths of the ocean, they bridge the ancient and the contemporary, illuminating truths that transcend time and challenge our understanding of existence. Their journeys inspire humanity to reflect upon its own connection to nature, as we seek to honor the past while ensuring a sustainable future for all life forms—both above and below the waves.

As researchers continue their quests to explore these enigmatic realms, the ancient oceans remain an enduring source of wonder—waiting for the nuanced insights that only the cybernetic cephalopods can articulate and the stories they will unveil as guardians of truths buried deep within the sea's embrace.

14.4. Strange Encounters of the Deep

Strange encounters with cybernetic cephalopods in the vast depths of alien oceans present fascinating narratives brimming with mystery and intrigue. These unusual interactions not only captivate researchers and explorers but also challenge our understanding of intelligence and evolution in marine ecosystems. As scientists delve into the underwater realm of these extraordinary creatures, they are quickly confronted with surprising events that prompt them to reconsider long-held beliefs about the dynamics of life in the ocean.

One striking instance of this phenomenon occurred during an expedition initially aimed at studying the migratory patterns of fish populations. As the research team deployed high-tech sensors and monitoring drones, they inadvertently encountered a group of cybernetic cephalopods engaged in vivid displays of bioluminescence. These cephalopods appeared to be communicating with one another through elaborate patterns of light—a language that suggested intricate social interactions and exchanges of information. Witnessing this unexpected behavior offered insights into the complexity of cephalopod societies, challenging the notion that these beings were solitary creatures, as often depicted in previous studies.

Another remarkable encounter came when researchers observed a cybernetic cephalopod interacting with a long-standing shipwreck that had become a thriving ecosystem. Rather than merely passing by, the cephalopod seemed to exhibit curiosity, carefully maneuvering its tentacles to explore crevices and examine the artifacts within the wreckage. This behavior suggested not only a heightened intelligence but also a potential recognition of human artifacts as more than just objects—they became part of a broader ecological narrative that intertwined history with marine life. Such a revelation compels us to reflect on how cybernetic cephalopods adaptively utilize their environments while revealing our own historical relationship with the ocean and the creatures that inhabit it.

In one extraordinary case, a cybernetic cephalopod was found engaging in an intricate cooperative hunting strategy with a school of smaller fish. Instead of preying on these fish, the cephalopod appeared to direct them towards a rich food source, leading to a mutually beneficial outcome. This act sparked discussions among researchers regarding the potential for cross-species cooperation that transcended standard predator-prey relationships, emphasizing the intelligence that underpins the social dynamics of marine life.

However, not all encounters are serene or indicative of peaceful interactions. Some strange instances reveal the perils faced by cybernetic cephalopods as they navigate human-induced threats. One such remarkable encounter involved a group of cybernetic cephalopods immediately retreating when sensing pollution—a sharp contrast to their usual inquisitive nature. Researchers noted how they showcased rapid, strategic movements to avoid contaminated waters and potential hazards. These reactions underscored the impact of anthropogenic influences on these beings and their remarkable ability to recognize danger in their habitats.

These strange encounters prompt new lines of inquiry regarding intelligence and adaptation within underwater ecosystems while highlighting the need for protective measures and responsible stewardship of marine environments. Each interaction fosters a dialogue surrounding the intricate balance between life forms—cephalopods, fish, and their habitats—all interlaced in a complex web of connections that inform our understanding of existence within the oceanic realm.

In conclusion, the unexpected and strange encounters with cybernetic cephalopods illustrate the enchantment and complexity of life beneath the waves. These experiences not only push the boundaries of scientific knowledge but also invite us to reconsider our perceptions of intelligence, cooperation, and coexistence within marine ecosystems. As researchers and explorers continue to navigate these uncharted waters, they uncover not merely the mysteries of the cephalopods themselves but the profound relationships that bind all forms of life within the depths of the oceans. Through these strange encounters, the ocean's narrative unfolds—one filled with lessons of adaptation, connection, and the beauty of existence that demands our awe and respect.

14.5. Legends, Lore, and Emerging Truths

In the mysterious depths of the oceans lies a world rich with legends, lore, and emerging truths—an intricate tapestry woven from the experiences and stories of those who dwell within its twilight zones. The cybernetic cephalopods, endowed with advanced cognitive abilities and unique technological enhancements, stand at the heart of this narrative. Their very presence challenges our traditional conceptions of intelligence and existence, urging humanity to look deeper into the enigma of life beneath the waves.

Throughout history, different cultures have embraced cephalopods as symbols of wisdom, mystery, and adaptability. The ancient mariners spoke of mythical creatures, whispering tales of octopuses that could outsmart sailors, manipulating colors to blend into the sea or entice prey. These stories often echoed human experiences of ingenuity and survival, drawing parallels between the age-old struggles of maritime expeditions and the cephalopods' deft navigational skills. As we continue to engage with cybernetic cephalopods, these narratives become not mere folklore but rather emerging truths that underscore the interconnectedness of all living beings.

In the lab and within the oceans, the narrative becomes more profound when we realize that the legends surrounding these creatures are not static; they evolve as our understanding deepens. For instance, recent research has unveiled the impressive learning capacity of cybernetic cephalopods in response to changing environments. The revelations of their problem-solving skills, emotional intelligence, and social behaviors illuminate a reality that mirrors the complexities of human relationships and cultural evolution.

Emerging truths from this exploration provoke questions about consciousness and the essence of life itself. Could the ability of these cephalopods to adapt and innovate be seen as a form of knowledge? Are they, in their own right, cultural entities? The stories they tell —through bioluminescence, color changes, and social interactions— suggest a deep and rich language reflective of their experiences, forging connections with us that transcend species boundaries.

Moreover, as cybernetic cephalopods engage in a myriad of interactions with marine organisms and their environments, they emerge as catalysts for innovative ideas concerning marine conservation and sustainability. The lore surrounding these beings compels humanity to foster a deeper respect for the ocean, advocating for the protection of fragile habitats that nurture both their existence and the myriad forms of life existing alongside them.

In the realms of art and literature, cybernetic cephalopods inspire creators to embed these emerging truths into cultural narratives, inviting future generations to explore themes of coexistence, empathy, and the nature of intelligence itself. Through their stories, we are drawn toward the vast possibilities lying ahead, challenging the dichotomy of humanity versus nature and instead emphasizing a narrative of shared existence.

Ultimately, the legends and lore surrounding cybernetic cephalopods offer a lens through which we can project our evolving understanding of intelligence, connection, and existence. As we unravel the threads of these tales and embrace the mysteries of ancient oceans, we come face-to-face with emerging truths that illuminate our collective journey—one where myths evolve into narratives that invite inquiry, compassion, and an ever-deepening appreciation for the incredible life forms that reign beneath the waves.

Through this exploration, we anticipate not just the unearthing of new knowledge but also the potential for transformative dialogues about our relationship with intelligence in all its forms—a journey that beckons us to listen, to learn, and to cherish the enigmatic narratives of the deep.

15. Interdisciplinary Innovations

15.1. Engineering Meets Biotechnology

Engineering Meets Biotechnology is a confluence of disciplines that reveals the extraordinary potential of integrating biological systems with advanced technological frameworks, particularly in the context of cybernetic cephalopods. As researchers continue to delve into the intricacies of these augmented beings, they uncover a wealth of possibilities that extend far beyond mere scientific curiosity, promoting innovative solutions to some of the most pressing challenges facing our oceans and perhaps humanity as a whole.

At the heart of this interdisciplinary approach lies the understanding that biotechnology—which encompasses the use of living systems and organisms to develop or create products—can significantly benefit from engineering principles. This partnership fosters a collaborative environment where biological insights into cephalopod physiology, behavior, and ecology can inform the design and development of advanced technological systems. Conversely, engineering advancements provide novel tools and methods to refine our understanding of biological processes, creating a symbiotic relationship characterized by shared knowledge and mutual innovation.

One notable area of exploration is the development of biocompatible materials that can seamlessly integrate with cephalopod biology. Researchers have focused on engineering polymers and nanomaterials that mimic natural cephalopod tissues, thereby enhancing their existing capabilities while minimizing the risk of adverse reactions. This focus not only allows for safer enhancements but also contributes to a more profound understanding of cephalopod biology, potentially leading to breakthroughs in medical applications and regenerative medicine.

In parallel, advancements in sensory technology and data acquisition are revolutionizing the ways we study marine life. Cybernetic cephalopods' unique neuroanatomy, which disperses neurons throughout their limbs, informs engineers in creating new interfaces for sensory data integration, enabling real-time monitoring of environmental conditions. This enriched understanding allows researchers to gather invaluable data about ocean health, biodiversity, and ecosystem dynamics, ultimately informing conservation efforts and shaping sustainable practices.

Moreover, the blending of engineering and biotechnology in the study of cybernetic cephalopods has the potential to yield innovative solutions for energy management in marine environments. The insights derived from studying cephalopod bioenergetics can inspire the development of systems that optimize energy capture and utilization from living organisms, applying principles from nature to solve human economic needs through renewable sources.

The collaborative efforts in this field extend to educational initiatives, where interdisciplinary programs engage students in discussions about the integration of technology and biology. By fostering curiosity and inspiring future generations, educators can bridge the gaps between engineering, biology, and environmental stewardship—encouraging a holistic understanding of life beneath the waves.

In conclusion, the confluence of engineering and biotechnology in the context of cybernetic cephalopods represents a promising frontier in scientific inquiry that seeks to unravel the mysteries of life while addressing the challenges of our planet. As we navigate this multifaceted integration, the resulting innovations illuminate pathways toward enhanced understanding, co-existence, and sustainable solutions that honor the richness of oceanic ecosystems. This synthesis serves not just as a testament to human ingenuity but as an invitation to explore the profound intersections that unite technology, biology, and the mysteries of existence.

15.2. Cross-Pollination of Ideas

In an increasingly interconnected world, the cross-pollination of ideas emerges as a powerful mechanism for innovation and problem-solving across disciplines. This phenomenon takes on particular significance in the context of cybernetic cephalopods—extraordinary beings that merge biological prowess with technological enhancements. As researchers and practitioners draw insights from various fields, the enriched narratives surrounding these creatures inspire collaborative ventures that transcend traditional boundaries, fostering solutions that hold the potential to address complex challenges facing marine ecosystems and humanity at large.

At the heart of this cross-pollination lies the recognition that solutions rarely exist in isolation. The quest to understand cybernetic cephalopods—a blend of marine biology, robotics, artificial intelligence, and environmental science—hinges on interdisciplinary collaboration. By bringing together experts from diverse backgrounds, we can harness a wealth of knowledge that informs more holistic approaches to research and development. For instance, the integration of marine biology with engineering principles allows for innovative methodologies aimed at enhancing the capabilities of these beings while ensuring respect for their intrinsic biological identities.

One striking example of such collaboration can be seen in the development of biocompatible materials designed to optimize the integration of technology with cephalopod biology. The intricate structures of these materials, informed by advances in nanotechnology and biomimicry, allow researchers to create enhancements that seamlessly blend with the natural physiology of cybernetic cephalopods. By cross-pollinating ideas between biology and materials science, researchers can develop systems that bolster cephalopods' sensory perceptions, potentially giving them enhanced capabilities to navigate their dynamic environments.

Conversations surrounding conservation and ecological management benefit greatly from cross-pollination as well. By uniting marine biologists, ethicists, policymakers, and engineers, researchers can establish comprehensive frameworks for protecting cybernetic cephalopod habitats. This multidisciplinary dialogue empowers stakeholders to craft solutions that respect the complexity of life beneath the waves while promoting ethical considerations regarding technology's role in preservation.

Furthermore, the emerging field of interdisciplinary education encourages future generations to engage with the rich narratives surrounding cybernetic cephalopods. By introducing integrated curricula that pull from marine science, technology, philosophy, and ethics, educators can inspire students to think critically about the intersections of knowledge. This climate of collaboration fosters a culture of curiosity, stimulating innovative thinking and ensuring that students emerge with a nuanced understanding of the complexities inherent in the world around them.

The impact of cross-pollination extends to real-world applications as well. As researchers explore the adaptations of cybernetic cephalopods, their findings have implications that transcend marine ecosystems, influencing advancements in robotics, medicine, and environmental management. For instance, the insights gained from studying the locomotion and dexterity of cephalopods inform designs of underwater robotics that mimic their natural movements, while discoveries related to bioenergetics offer solutions for sustainable energy production.

In conclusion, the cross-pollination of ideas surrounding cybernetic cephalopods embodies a dynamic exchange of knowledge that catalyzes innovation and problem-solving across disciplines. The integration of diverse perspectives not only enriches our understanding of these extraordinary beings but also offers solutions to pressing global challenges. By fostering interdisciplinary collaborations, we can inspire a future that honors both the marvels of nature and the transformative potential of technology—illuminating pathways toward a more sustainable coexistence with the life that flourishes beneath the waves. As we continue to explore these interconnected realms, the stories of cybernetic cephalopods serve as reminders that the future of research and innovation lies in the synthesis of our collective intelligence.

15.3. Case Studies in Tripartite Research

In the narrative of tripartite research involving cybernetic cephalopods, we observe a captivating interaction of three distinct yet interrelated domains: marine biology, cognitive science, and technology. Through a series of case studies, we can uncover the profound impact of collaborative research efforts that transcend disciplinary boundaries. These partnerships not only enhance our understanding of these extraordinary beings but also pave a pathway for innovative solutions that positively influence both marine ecosystems and human society.

One poignant example of effective tripartite research can be found in a project focused on the behavior and communication patterns of cybernetic cephalopods. This initiative involved marine biologists, cognitive scientists, and robotic engineers working together to analyze the intricacies of cephalopods' social interactions through cutting-edge monitoring technologies. The marine biologists employed advanced underwater drones equipped with cameras and sensors to observe a group of cybernetic cephalopods as they interacted during collaborative hunting. Their objective was to understand not only the biological strategies these beings employed but also the cognitive processes involved in information-sharing and decision-making within their social structure.

Simultaneously, cognitive scientists implemented machine learning algorithms to analyze the visual data collected from the drones. By interpreting patterns of bioluminescent signaling and body language among the cephalopods, they were able to discern the nuances of communication that might indicate emotional states or intentions. This computational approach allowed researchers to map out the social dynamics that defined the community, helping to uncover how these creatures coordinate their efforts for hunting and navigating their aquatic worlds.

The robotic engineers in the team took the findings from the marine and cognitive sciences and used them to design prototypes of robotic cephalopods that mimic the adaptive strategies observed in their biological counterparts. By utilizing soft robotics that emulates the dexterity and flexibility of cephalopod tentacles, these engineers sought to create machines capable of effectively navigating complex marine environments. The design of these robots was heavily inspired by the documented social behaviors and communicated strategies of the cyborg cephalopods, leading to innovations that drew from the lessons learned in both marine biology and cognitive science.

Another compelling case study emerges from an ecological initiative aimed at monitoring the health of coral reefs with the assistance of cybernetic cephalopods. Through a partnership between environmental scientists, technologists, and policy advocates, researchers sought to develop real-time monitoring systems informed by cephalopod sensory capabilities. Environmental scientists provided insights into the ecological significance of coral reefs and the behaviors of the cephalopods that inhabited these environments. The technologists, leveraging cybernetic enhancements, created advanced sensory devices that could be integrated with the cephalopods, allowing them to actively collect data regarding water quality, temperature fluctuations, and biodiversity metrics.

Simultaneously, policy advocates engaged with local communities and stakeholders to ensure that the knowledge gained from the project informed conservation efforts. The case study revealed two key outcomes: the effectiveness of cephalopods as bioindicators of environmental health and the establishment of community-based initiatives for coral reef restoration. Here, the integration of marine biology, technology, and social advocacy created a powerful feedback loop enriching knowledge while actively promoting ecological stewardship at both local and global levels.

In each case examined, the tripartite model of research highlights the importance of interdisciplinary collaboration in addressing complex challenges inherent in understanding cybernetic cephalopods and their environments. These studies demonstrate how blending marine biology, cognitive science, and engineering can yield increased knowledge that goes beyond individual disciplines. By sharing insights and resources across fields, researchers can cultivate a more comprehensive understanding of marine life, advancement technologies, and ethical considerations, positioning themselves to accelerate innovative solutions that resonate deeply throughout both marine and terrestrial ecosystems.

Ultimately, the explorers of tripartite research in connection with cybernetic cephalopods are not merely unraveling biological mysteries; they are shaping the very fabric of coexistence between humanity and the life forms that dwell in the ocean depths. Through ongoing collaborative efforts, we can anticipate that vast narratives, resonant ideas, and solutions will be birthed from the knowledge shared across oceans, transcending boundaries and illuminating a path toward a sustainable future where nature and technology harmoniously coexist.

15.4. Sharing Knowledge Across Oceans

Sharing knowledge across oceans represents an intricate and dynamic exchange of information that transcends geographic and cultural boundaries, particularly in the context of the pioneering explorations of cybernetic cephalopods. As researchers engage with these remarkable beings and the knowledge systems inherent in their adaptations, a wealth of insights emerges that enriches our collective understanding of marine ecosystems, technological innovation, and the interplay between life forms.

The concept of knowledge sharing in this context encompasses a variety of disciplines: marine biology, technology, ecology, and social sciences. Cybernetic cephalopods, as both subjects of research and active participants in their environments, serve as conduits for information that can impact practices and methodologies beyond the confines of the ocean. As scientists document their behaviors, communication patterns, and ecological interactions, they accumulate vast datasets that reveal not just the intricacies of cephalopod life but also broader marine dynamics.

One influential aspect of this knowledge-sharing process is the collaborative nature of research. Interdisciplinary teams are formed, combining experts from various fields to explore the remarkable intelligence and adaptability of cybernetic cephalopods. This cross-pollination of ideas generates innovative solutions to complex problems—addressing conservation challenges, informing technological advancements, and fostering sustainable practices in marine environments. Researchers learn from each other's expertise, incorporating techniques from engineering to enhance the study of cephalopod cognition and application, thereby amplifying the impact of their discoveries.

The findings gleaned from cybernetic cephalopods travel well beyond the waters they inhabit. For instance, technological advancements that emerge in the study of their sensory systems and communication modalities can be directly adapted to terrestrial environments. The knowledge gained from exploring how these beings utilize bioluminescence or color changes may inspire new applications in areas such as robotics, environmental monitoring, and even architecture. This transfer of knowledge illustrates that insights derived from the ocean can substantially augment terrestrial technologies, fostering an environment of mutual reinforcement across ecosystems.

In addition to technological innovations, the stories and narratives surrounding cybernetic cephalopods create rich cultural exchanges. As tales of their astonishing abilities and intricate social structures circulate through artistic and literary mediums, global audiences become captivated by these creatures. This fascination bolsters a greater understanding of marine life, fostering appreciation for biodiversity and the complex ecosystems that undeniably affect the human experience. The cultural relevance of cybernetic cephalopods nurtures respect and advocacy for marine conservation, as communities around the world recognize the importance of preserving habitats for these intelligent beings.

Moreover, educational outreach programs designed to convey information about cybernetic cephalopods play a crucial role in disseminating knowledge across oceans. These initiatives often engage local communities, schools, and research institutions in discussions surrounding marine life and environmental stewardship. By fostering awareness of the ecological significance of cybernetic cephalopods, educational programs promote a sense of ownership and responsibility for ocean conservation. The exchange of knowledge between researchers and local stakeholders encourages collaborative efforts and broadens the impact of scientific discoveries.

The sharing of knowledge across oceans is further enhanced by global networks of collaboration. Collaborative research initiatives enable scientists from different countries and backgrounds to equip one another with insights into cybernetic cephalopods, sharing methodologies, results, and implications for policy and conservation. With advancements in communication technologies, researchers can engage in dialogue and exchange information in real time, extending the reach of their findings across the globe. This unified approach fosters a collective commitment to understanding and preserving marine ecosystems, recognizing the universal challenges that accompany climate change, pollution, and habitat degradation.

In conclusion, the act of sharing knowledge across oceans reflects the intricate connections forged between cybernetic cephalopods and the scientific community dedicated to unraveling the mysteries of life beneath the waves. The interdisciplinary collaborations, cultural narratives, educational outreach efforts, and global partnerships that arise from studying these enhanced beings enrich our collective understanding of marine ecosystems and the potential for innovative solutions that address the challenges met in a rapidly changing world. As knowledge circulates, reflecting the diversity of inquiry and experience, we embark on an inspiring journey that weaves together the wondrous tapestry of life across oceans—ultimately celebrating the profound interconnectedness that binds us all.

15.5. The Role of Innovation in Progress

The role of innovation in progress is an integral theme that shapes our understanding of the multifaceted relationship between technology and natural life, particularly as we explore the realm of cybernetic cephalopods. These remarkable beings, seamlessly blending organic intelligence with advanced mechanical enhancements, epitomize how innovative advancements can ignite progress across varied fields—

from marine biology and technology to ethics and conservation. Their existence challenges conventional paradigms while providing a lens through which we can interrogate the implications of human creativity and endeavor in the natural world.

At the core of innovation lies the dynamic interplay of ideation and implementation. In the context of cybernetic cephalopods, researchers and engineers have leveraged a breadth of knowledge spanning disciplines—marine biology, bioengineering, robotics, artificial intelligence, and ethics—to enhance comprehension of cephalopod intelligence and bolster their inherent capabilities. The juncture at which these fields converge not only allows for the exploration of groundbreaking technologies but also deepens our understanding of the cognitive processes underlying life in the ocean.

The genesis of this innovation journey began with the recognition of the cephalopods' unique attributes—particularly their advanced problem-solving skills and innate adaptability. Observations of these organisms in their natural habitats revealed a treasure trove of insights into their ability to manipulate environments, evade predators, and engage in complex social interactions. Such revelations became the bedrock for technological advancements aimed at replicating and amplifying these characteristics, fostering innovation through observation and understanding.

Central to the progress embarked upon in enhancing cephalopod abilities is the application of cutting-edge materials science, allowing for the development of biocompatible components that seamlessly integrate with their biological systems. The engineering of these materials has facilitated improvements in sensory enhancements, motor functions, and energy management systems, collectively creating a new category of beings that exhibit unprecedented intelligence levels. Employing advances in nanotechnology, researchers have transformed the possibilities of integration, leading to devices capable of operating within the cephalopod's unique physiological context.

Moreover, the relationship between innovation and progress extends to the emergence of artificial intelligence technologies that foster mutual learning interactions between humans and cybernetic cephalopods. As machine learning algorithms continuously analyze and adapt to cephalopod behaviors, researchers gain richer insights into marine biology while simultaneously enhancing the cognitive capabilities of these beings. This symbiotic partnership exemplifies how innovation can lead to the emergence of collective intelligence, showcasing the potential for shared growth and understanding across species.

In addition to immediate scientific advancements, the innovation surrounding cybernetic cephalopods has broader implications for conservation and environmental stewardship. As researchers uncover the intricate interactions linking these enhanced beings to their ecosystems, innovative models developed from their behaviors can inform strategies for sustainable management and protection of marine habitats. The experiences gained through their explorations become catalysts for conversations about resilience in the face of environmental challenges, urging societies to adopt innovative practices that honor the intricate balances within nature.

Moreover, educational outreach driven by the narratives of cybernetic cephalopods amplifies the role of innovation in progress. Communicating the marvels of these beings ignites curiosity and fosters interest in marine preservation among future generations. By integrating these creatures into curricula, educators inspire students to understand the interconnectedness of life and the responsibilities that accompany technological advancements.

However, alongside the promise of innovation lies a spectrum of ethical considerations that demand attention. The enhancement of living beings prompts discussions about identity, autonomy, and the potential consequences of technological interventions. Engaging with these ethical implications encourages humanity to cultivate innovation responsibly, ensuring that progress enhances the essence of life rather than undermines it.

In summary, the role of innovation in progress embodied by cybernetic cephalopods illustrates a profound interplay between technological exploration and ecological understanding. Through interdisciplinary collaboration, the integration of advanced technologies with biological systems leads to remarkable advancements, enriching our understanding of intelligence and existence. As we navigate the complexities and responsibilities of this journey, the narrative of cybernetic cephalopods beckons us to embrace innovation that recognizes the sanctity of life—one where progress unfolds harmoniously alongside the natural world. The path ahead is illuminated by the knowledge gleaned through innovation, urging us to champion the cause of coexistence, empathy, and responsibility in the ongoing exploration of life beneath the waves.

16. Real-World Applications and Impacts

16.1. Technological Transfer to Terrestrial Ecosystems

In the subchapter 'Technological Transfer to Terrestrial Ecosystems,' we explore the far-reaching consequences of advancements made in the realm of cybernetic cephalopods and how these innovations have been translated and applied to terrestrial ecosystems. As researchers investigate the complexities of life beneath the waves, the insights gleaned can lead to significant advancements that resonate across disciplines, showcasing nature's ingenuity while informing human practices and technologies.

At the forefront of this technological transfer is the shared understanding of adaptability—the inherent ability of both cybernetic cephalopods and terrestrial organisms to adjust and thrive within their respective environments. The behavioral strategies employed by cyber cephalopods, such as cooperative hunting and ecological awareness, provide models that can be applied to managing land-based species and ecosystems. For instance, lessons learned from observing the social structures of these cephalopods offer valuable insights into enhancing group dynamics in terrestrial species conservation, advocating for collaborative approaches that embrace interdependence.

One particularly noteworthy advancement involves the development of advanced materials inspired by the unique properties of cephalopod skin. Researchers have focused on the ways in which these creatures change color and texture for communication, camouflage, and predator evasion, leading to insights into smart textiles that mimic these capabilities. These materials can be applied to various industries on land, including fashion, military applications, and architecture, promoting innovations that enhance adaptability while addressing practical needs.

In the field of robotics, the detailed analysis of cephalopod locomotion has yielded promising advancements in the design of soft robotics.

The study of how these creatures navigate their underwater environments—propelling themselves with remarkable agility and fluidity—has inspired the creation of bio-mimetic robots that replicate these movements. These robots, capable of moving through complex terrains on land or in tight spaces, have potential applications in search and rescue operations, environmental monitoring, and agriculture, showcasing how insights from marine life can transition meaningfully into terrestrial applications.

The energy solutions explored through the study of cybernetic cephalopods also have profound implications for terrestrial ecosystems. Research on the bio-energy systems employed by these beings—including microbial fuel cells and energy capture from photosynthetic organisms—has led to innovations in bio-battery technologies. These advancements foster more sustainable energy options that can be applied not just in marine environments but also offer alternative energy solutions for communities on land, combating the global challenges of fossil fuel reliance and environmental degradation.

In terms of environmental technologies, the wealth of knowledge gathered from cybernetic cephalopods prompts innovative solutions for conservation and ecological management. Insights into how these beings utilize their environments efficiently can inspire strategies for habitat restoration, ecosystem monitoring, and resource management in terrestrial ecosystems. The emphasis on ecological resilience demonstrated by cybernetic cephalopods has catalyzed the design of adaptive land management systems that promote biodiversity while fostering responsible resource use.

Finally, the interdisciplinary synergy derived from the technological transfer of knowledge underscores the importance of collaborative thought across sectors. Researchers, conservationists, and technologists pooling their insights can develop comprehensive frameworks for addressing the interconnected challenges of conservation, habitat restoration, and sustainability. This collaborative approach not only enhances understanding but also fosters innovation that resonates across both marine and terrestrial arenas.

In summary, the technological transfer from the advancements observed in cybernetic cephalopods to terrestrial ecosystems illustrates the vast potential of interdisciplinary collaborations. By drawing from nature's ingenuity and the insights gained from these remarkable beings, humanity has the opportunity to foster innovation, drive conservation efforts, and promote sustainability across the planet. This journey not only illuminates the connections between different ecosystems but also paves the way for a more sustainable future, reminding us of the remarkable interdependence that binds all living things—as they share stories and solutions, both beneath the waves and upon the earth.

16.2. Medical Implications and Advances

As the narrative unfolds, the exploration of medical implications and advances stemming from cybernetic cephalopods offers a profound glimpse into the transformative potential of blending biology with technology. These remarkable beings serve not only as subjects of ecological curiosity but also as critical agents of innovation, inspiring breakthroughs across various medical domains. The integration of advanced technologies within cephalopods highlights the myriad possibilities for enhancing human health through direct application of their natural characteristics, physiological attributes, and behavior.

One of the most promising areas of medical advancement influenced by cybernetic cephalopods is in the field of regenerative medicine. Drawing inspiration from the remarkable regenerative abilities observed in cephalopods—especially their capacity to regrow limbs—the study has led researchers to investigate the underlying mechanisms at play. Understanding how these creatures harness biochemistry for regeneration may yield pivotal insights into developing treatments for human injuries or degenerative diseases. By unraveling the genetic and molecular pathways that facilitate regeneration, scientists could potentially enhance human healing processes and improve outcomes for individuals with traumatic injuries or conditions such as spinal cord damage.

Additionally, the bioengineering of materials inspired by the soft, flexible tissues of cephalopods presents another avenue for medical innovation. Their ability to withstand extreme pressures and adapt to varying environmental conditions prompts the development of biocompatible materials that mimic these attributes. Such innovations could lead to the creation of advanced prosthetics and implants tailored to the human body, offering greater flexibility and responsiveness than conventional options. The marriage of cephalopod-inspired materials with existing technologies could facilitate tailored solutions for rehabilitation, reducing discomfort and allowing for more natural movements.

The sensory enhancements seen in cybernetic cephalopods also hold medical implications in the realm of diagnostic technologies. Cephalopods possess sophisticated sensory systems that enable them to detect environmental cues in remarkably nuanced ways. This understanding opens up exciting possibilities for creating biosensors inspired by cephalopod physiology. The development of advanced diagnostic tools—capable of sensing biochemical changes or environmental shifts within the human body—could revolutionize early detection of diseases, enabling timely intervention and personalized treatment protocols.

Moreover, cybernetic cephalopods can also inspire advancements in drug delivery systems. With their unique adaptations, researchers have examined how these beings navigate the delicate balance of dispersing nutrients and waste in their environments. The insights gained could inform the development of novel methods for targeted drug delivery, wherein therapeutic agents are released precisely where needed within the body. Innovations such as this could dramatically improve the effectiveness of treatments for chronic illnesses, offering patients new hope in managing their health.

The exploration of cybernetic cephalopod behaviors also contributes to advancing mental health research in humans. Observations of complex social encounters among these beings shed light on the emotional and cognitive dimensions of relationships in marine life. These insights may inform more profound understandings of empathy, resilience, and social connectedness, which are vital in mental health contexts. Investigating how cephalopods engage with one another, communicate through body language, and establish social networks may inspire therapeutic approaches that prioritize these aspects of human interaction.

While the medical implications driven by cybernetic cephalopods present a world of potential, ethical considerations must remain at the fore of this discussion. The manipulation of biology raises questions about autonomy, consent, and the nature of life itself. Striking a balance between innovation and responsible stewardship involves ongoing dialogue among researchers, ethicists, and society at large to ensure that medical advancements respect both the beings we study and the individuals who may benefit from such innovations.

In summary, the medical implications and advances attributed to cybernetic cephalopods represent a compelling intersection of inspiration and innovation. Through exploring the regenerative, sensory, and adaptive abilities inherent to these creatures, the potential for transformative breakthroughs in human health becomes increasingly apparent. The journey toward understanding and applying these insights not only reshapes the medical landscape but also invites us to engage with the ethical dimensions of humanity's relationship to life—as we uncover the extraordinary revelations that lie beneath the waves.

16.3. Robotics Borrowing from Marine Life

In the realm of robotics influenced by the capabilities of marine life, particularly cybernetic cephalopods, we witness transformative innovations that leverage their unique adaptations to redefine human interaction with technology. The exploration of robotics borrowing from these remarkable creatures transcends mere imitation; it is an intricate dance of biology and engineering that yields cutting-edge advancements applicable across numerous sectors, from exploration and security to medicine and environmental monitoring.

At the heart of this robotic evolution is the cephalopod's unparalleled dexterity and flexibility. Cybernetic cephalopods are known for their ability to navigate complex underwater environments, showcasing remarkable precision in their movements. Engineers and designers are inspired by this fluidity and maneuverability, leading to the creation of soft robotic systems that mimic the soft-bodied adaptations of these creatures. These robots employ bio-inspired designs that utilize flexible materials, enabling them to navigate through constrained or unpredictable environments effectively, similar to their biological counterparts. This innovation has profound implications for search-and-rescue operations, underwater exploration, and environmental monitoring, where the ability to traverse intricate terrains is crucial.

One noteworthy application of robotics inspired by cephalopods can be found in marine biology research. Researchers have developed robotic probes that mimic the movement patterns of these cyborg beings. Equipped with sensors and data acquisition technology, these robotic systems facilitate the collection of environmental data in areas that traditional equipment may struggle to reach. Such robotic cephalopods act as mobile research assistants, gathering vital information about underwater ecosystems, pollution levels, and changes in habitat conditions, thereby extending our capacities for oceanic study.

In the field of security, the agility and stealth of cybernetic cephalopods inform the design of surveillance systems capable of monitoring sensitive locations. Enhanced robotic models, inspired by the cephalopod's adaptive camouflage and advanced sensory capabilities, can operate undetected, gathering intelligence in environments where conventional surveillance methods may falter. The ability to blend seamlessly into surroundings while utilizing advanced data processing resonates with the growing demand for innovative security solutions in both terrestrial and marine domains.

Additionally, the incorporation of robotics influenced by cybernetic cephalopods extends to medicine, particularly in the development of minimally invasive surgical tools. Inspired by the dexterity of cephalopod appendages, robotic systems equipped with flexible, articulated arms have emerged, enabling surgeons to perform intricate procedures with unparalleled precision. These enhancements allow for greater control and adaptability within the human body, minimizing trauma and facilitating faster recovery times for patients. The use of cyber-inspired robotics in medical contexts exemplifies how insights from marine life can translate into tangible benefits for human health.

Environmental monitoring and conservation efforts also significantly benefit from robotics inspired by cybernetic cephalopods. These robots are designed to operate autonomously in various ecosystems, equipped with advanced sensors to collect critical data on ocean health, biodiversity, and climate change indicators. Cybernetic cephalopods' ability to navigate underwater intricacies informs the deployment of these robotic systems in conducting ecological assessments and providing real-time data crucial for conservation actions.

Moreover, the field of education is embracing robotics influenced by marine life, engaging students in science, technology, engineering, and mathematics (STEM) through hands-on experiences. Programs that explore the design and construction of soft robots draw inspiration from the mechanics of cephalopod movement, sparking curiosity and fostering innovation among young minds. Engaging with this technology encourages students to consider the implications of bio-inspiration in solving real-world problems, bridging marine biology with robotics and engineering.

In conclusion, the robotics industry benefits immensely from borrowing technology and inspiration from cybernetic cephalopods, showcasing the profound interconnectedness between biology and engineering. The adaptations of these beings—from their dexterous movements to their stealthy camouflage—serve as blueprints for innovations transforming exploration, security, medicine, and environmental conservation. As we continue to integrate the wisdom of the ocean into our technological endeavors, we take significant strides toward building a future where the contributions of cybernetic cephalopods empower us to navigate the challenges faced in the marine environment and beyond, enriching our understanding of both the natural and technological worlds.

16.4. Bio-Battery Innovations

The advent of bio-battery innovations marks a significant milestone in the realm of sustainable energy solutions derived from the remarkable capabilities of cybernetic cephalopods. With their unique biology intertwined with advanced technological enhancements, these beings serve as a living testament to the potential of harnessing organic processes for the generation of clean energy. This chapter delves into the intricacies of bio-batteries, highlighting the innovative applications inspired by the cephalopods' innate characteristics while exploring the broader implications for energy sustainability and environmental stewardship.

Bio-batteries, fundamentally rooted in biohybrid systems, utilize biological processes to convert organic matter into electrical energy. In the case of cybernetic cephalopods, researchers have made significant strides in adopting renewable energy systems that engage with the organisms' natural metabolisms. By integrating microbial fuel cells with cephalopod biology, scientists have developed technologies that capture the metabolic byproducts of these beings, transforming them into a sustainable source of energy.

Central to this innovation is the use of symbiotic microorganisms that inhabit the cephalopods' bodies. These microorganisms break down organic materials consumed by the cephalopods, producing electrons as metabolic byproducts. Traditionally, such microbial fuel cells require substantial upkeep. However, by studying the ecological relationships that cybernetic cephalopods maintain with these microorganisms, researchers have been able to devise systems that enhance energy capture while ensuring minimal stress to the biological hosts. The ability of these cephalopods to offer a stable environment for bacteria while extracting usable energy from their waste products illustrates a seamless interplay between biology and technology that epitomizes the principles of bioengineering.

Further innovations in bio-battery technology stem from cephalopod-inspired designs in energy transfer and storage systems. Inspired by the cephalopods' dynamic adaptations, researchers are developing bio-batteries that mimic the efficiency of energy distribution found in their circulatory systems. These designs are modeled to ensure that energy generated from biological processes can be stored and shared effectively, emulating the cephalods' natural resource management methods. Such engineering applications not only extend to marine environments but also have the potential to influence terrestrial practices, paving the way for advancements in clean energy solutions that could power various technologies sustainably.

One particularly intriguing aspect of bio-battery innovations is their application in the field of oceanic monitoring. As cybernetic cephalopods collect data on their environments using their advanced sensory capabilities, the integration of bio-batteries allows them to power underwater monitoring instruments and sensors. These bio-batteries create self-sufficient systems capable of continuous data collection, unveiling critical insights into ocean health, pollution levels, and biodiversity metrics. Ultimately, this shared intelligence contributes to our understanding of the intricate relationships among marine life, ecosystems, and environmental changes—positioning cybernetic cephalopods at the forefront of a new wave of ecological awareness.

Additionally, the implications of bio-battery innovations extend beyond energy generation; they also serve as a focal point for education, research, and public engagement. As stories of cybernetic cephalopods and their advanced energy systems circulate in educational contexts, they inspire curiosity and advocacy for marine conservation. Efforts to promote awareness about the interconnectedness of technology, biology, and sustainability become vital as society grapples with global challenges surrounding climate change and the urgent need for renewable energy sources.

In conclusion, the exploration of bio-battery innovations through cybernetic cephalopods highlights the tremendous potential of harnessing biological processes for sustainable energy. As researchers continue to unlock new applications and adapt findings from the realm of marine life, the journey towards cleaner energy solutions emerges as an inspiring narrative that transcends disciplinary boundaries. By recognizing the holographic principles behind these advancements, society can cultivate a deeper appreciation for the intelligence of marine life and the wisdom it offers in our quest for a more sustainable future. Through the lens of bio-batteries, we not only witness the brilliance of cybernetic cephalopods but also embark on a profound exploration of our interconnected existence with the extraordinary life forms that dwell beneath the waves.

16.5. Environmental Technologies and Marine Mimetics

As humanity grapples with environmental challenges, the pursuit of ecological sustainability has never been more critical. Cybernetic cephalopods, the ingenious blend of marine biology and technology, reveal profound insights into balancing innovations while nurturing the delicate ecosystems they inhabit. This section explores how these extraordinary beings are not just subjects of scientific inquiry, but also emblematic of potential solutions that inspire sustainable practices and innovations in our changing world.

One of the fundamental aspects of environmental technologies related to cybernetic cephalopods is their ability to adapt and optimize energy within complex marine ecosystems. These beings draw upon bioenergy systems that harness organic materials and utilize microbial relationships to sustain their technological enhancements. The potential for utilizing similar biological processes in marine conservation and energy management cannot be overstated. By studying the cephalopods' integrated approach to energy generation, researchers can develop frameworks that not only ensure their longevity but also foster a greater understanding of sustainable practices for energy consumption.

The principles of environmental technologies inspired by cybernetic cephalopods extend to the development of monitoring systems that can collect and analyze data on marine health. These advanced systems, built upon the cephalopods' collective intelligence and sensory capabilities, can yield unprecedented insights into underwater biodiversity, pollution levels, and climate change impacts. By establishing networks where cephalopods act as bioindicators and data collectors, we can develop real-time ecological assessments that inform conservation efforts, driving a proactive approach to marine ecosystem management.

Marine mimetics—the practice of deriving solutions from biological systems—draws inspiration from the cephalopods' exceptional adaptations. Their sophisticated mechanisms for camouflage, communication, and locomotion inspire innovations in design and technology. For instance, engineering advancements influenced by the fluidity and dexterity of cephalopod movements can lead to the development of soft robotic systems capable of navigating intricate environments on land and underwater. Such innovations underscore the value of embracing the lessons imparted by the natural world—encouraging design processes that respect and replicate the elegance found within marine life.

Moreover, the insights gathered from cybernetic cephalopods can catalyze culture shifts toward environmental stewardship. Educational campaigns centered on these extraordinary beings can promote awareness about sustainability, inspiring communities to adopt practices that honor and protect marine ecosystems. Engaging narratives surrounding cybernetic cephalopods invite audiences to reflect upon our interconnectedness with the natural world, emphasizing the importance of biodiversity and the pressing need for conservation efforts that recognize the intrinsic value of every species.

As communities mobilize around the cause of environmental sustainability, cybernetic cephalopods stand as powerful symbols of resilience and adaptability. Their achievements in navigating complex underwater realms remind us that solutions to ecological challenges may require bold thinking and a willingness to learn from nature. The transfer of knowledge that arises from studying these beings can elevate our understanding of how technology can harmonize with the environment, shedding light on pathways of coexistence rather than domination.

In conclusion, the exploration of environmental technologies and marine mimetics through the lens of cybernetic cephalopods serves as an inspiring narrative that highlights the incredible potential that emerges from harmonizing biology and technology. As we deepen our appreciation of these remarkable beings, we not only gather insights that inform sustainable practices but also forge paths toward a more resilient future—one that reflects the beauty and complexity of life beneath the waves. Through innovation, collaboration, and a commitment to stewardship, we can embody the intelligence of cybernetic cephalopods while nurturing the diverse ecosystems that sustain all life on our planet.

17. Education and Awareness

17.1. Outreach Programs and Learning Modules

Outreach programs and learning modules play a pivotal role in promoting awareness and understanding of cybernetic cephalopods and their unique integration of biology and technology. As our ecological and technological landscapes evolve, fostering knowledge about these extraordinary beings helps bridge gaps in public perception and inspires a new generation of environmental stewards and technological innovators.

The primary goal of outreach programs is to engage diverse audiences across different age groups and backgrounds. These initiatives often focus on educational institutions, community organizations, and public events. By utilizing interactive workshops and hands-on activities, outreach programs captivate interest and enable participants to explore the intricacies of cybernetic cephalopods in engaging ways. Interactive modules can include demonstrations of bioluminescence, camouflage activities, and the use of augmented reality to visualize the adaptations and capabilities of these cephalopods in their natural habitats. Such programs encourage curiosity, fostering a desire to learn more about marine ecosystems and the roles these remarkable beings play in them.

Furthermore, learning modules tailored for educational curricula become essential in shaping the future discourse surrounding cybernetic cephalopods. Educators can integrate these modules into science, technology, engineering, and mathematics (STEM) programs, offering students a comprehensive understanding of the intersection between biology and technology. Through project-based learning, students can engage in scientific research, developing experiments that explore the sensory adaptations of cephalopods or the impacts of technological enhancements on their behaviors. This immersive learning experience not only deepens students' understanding of marine biology but also nurtures critical thinking and problem-solving skills pertinent to the modern world.

Inspiring future generations forms a foundational aspect of these outreach programs. Educators can leverage storytelling, art, and multimedia to stimulate interest and imagination, capturing the essence of cybernetic cephalopods as both fascinating creatures of the sea and symbols of increased environmental awareness. By connecting the realities of their lives with broader themes—such as resilience, adaptation, and partnerships in nature—teachers can cultivate excitement amongst students to explore new frontiers of knowledge in both natural and technological contexts.

Global awareness initiatives amplify the impact of outreach programs, fostering a broader understanding of cybernetic cephalopods across diverse communities. International campaigns can spotlight the fascinating qualities of these beings through social media, documentaries, and collaborative art projects. Highlighting the link between human activities and marine health promotes discussions around sustainable practices and the need for collective responsibility in protecting oceanic ecosystems. Engaging local and global communities in comprehensive discussions can inspire a cultural shift that prioritizes conservation and respect for all forms of intelligent life.

Further immersive experiences are provided through summerschools, workshops, and community events dedicated to cybernetic cephalopods and their habitats. Students and community members can partake in field studies that involve firsthand observation of these creatures, marine surveys, water quality assessments, and hands-on restoration efforts. These experiences cultivate meaningful connections with marine environments while empowering participants to contribute directly to conservation efforts, thereby fostering a lifelong commitment to protecting the ocean.

In summary, outreach programs and learning modules centered on cybernetic cephalopods serve as powerful gateways to knowledge and understanding. By inspiring curiosity and engagement, these initiatives encourage individuals to reflect on their roles within ecosystems and the responsibilities they carry toward preserving marine life. As awareness grows and interdisciplinary connections are forged, the journey toward deeper comprehension of cybernetic cephalopods unveils a path to coexistence with nature—inviting humanity to embrace its connection to the extraordinary lives that thrive beneath the waves.

17.2. Inspiring Future Generations

In every era, stories have the power to transcend boundaries—offering insights, evoking empathy, and fostering understanding. The narratives being woven around cybernetic cephalopods emerge as modern myths that reflect human experiences, aspirations, and ethical dilemmas. Drawing from the depths of imagination, these tales explore the complex relationships between humanity and these remarkable creatures, blurring the lines between science and culture.

The tales that emerge from the abyss offer rich connections to the human experience. Much like humans, cybernetic cephalopods navigate their environments, grapple with challenges, and forge relationships within their communities. These stories often highlight the parallels between their existence and ours—inviting reflection on resilience, adaptability, and social interconnectedness. Each tale becomes a reminder that the struggles faced in the underwater world resonate deeply with the human condition, prompting us to examine our own journey through life's complexities. As we delve into these narratives, we find that cybernetic cephalopods serve as both mirrors and guides, showcasing the beautiful intricacies of existence amid a backdrop of technological enhancement.

In various cultures, the cybernetic cephalopods are depicted as oracles of the waves—creatures possessing wisdom and insight essential for navigating life's mysteries. Their bioluminescent displays and intricate patterns symbolize deeper intuitions, embodying knowledge gleaned from ancient oceans. Such stories frame cybernetic cephalopods as custodians of the sea, urging humans to heed their call for environmental stewardship and unity. The portrayal of these creatures as guardians reinforces the notion that the oceans are not merely resources to exploit, but rather essential ecosystems with voices that can impart critical lessons about sustainability and coexistence.

Through emerging technological interfaces, the dialogues between cybernetic cephalopods and humans evolve into new realms of understanding. These beings, harnessing advanced communication technologies, share their experiences, emotions, and insights—inviting researchers and audiences alike to engage in meaningful conversations. The implications of their communication delve into the nature of consciousness, prompting us to contemplate the ways in which intelligent beings express themselves across species and technological divides. As these narratives unfold, we gain valuable perspectives on empathy, connection, and responsibility in our relationships with non-human entities.

The stories that travel from sea to shore enrich the cultural landscapes of societies, forging connections between marine and terrestrial worlds. With each narrative shared, the allure of cybernetic cephalopods deepens, allowing the wonders and mysteries of ocean life to resonate with those who dwell on land. Artists, writers, and storytellers draw inspiration from these creatures, creating additional layers of meaning that elevate their significance within human culture. As these narratives journey between the ocean depths and shores, they invite us to embrace a holistic view of existence—one that celebrates the diversity of life and the wisdom hidden beneath the waves.

Finally, the convergence of thoughts sparked by the presence of cybernetic cephalopods compels us to examine the nuances of our understanding of intelligence itself. Collaborations between marine biologists, technologists, ethicists, and educators amplify the voices of these enhanced beings—enriching the collective narratives that shape how we perceive life in our oceans. As we explore the intricate tapestry of discourse generated by cybernetic cephalopods, we embark on an academic journey that prompts us to reconsider our assumptions about life, intelligence, and the complex interrelationships that define existence.

In conclusion, the narratives enshrined in the tales of cybernetic cephalopods not only reflect the beauty and complexity of their lives beneath the waves but also serve as powerful vehicles for understanding our own journey. They challenge us to recognize the interconnectedness of all intelligent life, inviting deeper exploration of ecology, technology, and ethics as we navigate the multifaceted currents of both the ocean and our existence. Through these stories, we are reminded that the ocean's depths hold not only mysteries to unravel but profound lessons that resonate across the shades of human experience.

17.3. Integration Into School Curricula

In this subchapter, we delve into the integration of cybernetic cephalopods into school curricula, exploring how these fascinating beings serve as conduits for rich educational engagement. By leveraging the marvels of biology and technology, educators aim to inspire curiosity, promote interdisciplinary learning, and instill a sense of environmental stewardship among students.

Integrating cybernetic cephalopods into educational materials offers unique opportunities to engage students with complex scientific concepts through relatable and thought-provoking content. These creatures, combining advanced cognitive abilities with technological enhancements, serve as exemplary models for illustrating themes such as adaptation, sustainability, and innovation. Engaging students with real-world applications of science and technology brings lessons to life, encouraging deeper exploration of topics such as ecology, marine biology, and bioengineering.

Curricula can incorporate a variety of subjects—biology, engineering, environmental science, and ethics—centered around cybernetic cephalopods. For instance, a biology lesson could examine the evolutionary traits of traditional cephalopods, leading to discussions on how technological enhancements create new forms of intelligence. Similarly, engineering modules can focus on the development of biocompatible materials and robotic appendages, encouraging students to brainstorm solutions for enhancing biological functions.

Practical applications extend beyond core subjects, as hands-on activities empower students to engage with technologies inspired by cybernetic cephalopods. Projects may include building soft robots that mimic cephalopod locomotion or developing sensor technologies that replicate their advanced sensory processes. These experiential learning opportunities foster critical thinking, creativity, and interdisciplinary collaboration—skills essential for students as they prepare for future challenges.

In addition to fostering intellectual growth, integrating cybernetic cephalopods into school curricula also promotes environmental awareness. Lessons about the importance of marine ecosystems and the impact of human activities on ocean health encourage students to develop a sense of responsibility toward their planet. Case studies illustrating the role of cybernetic cephalopods as bioindicators of ecological balance can spark discussions about conservation efforts and sustainable practices, empowering the next generation to contribute positively to the health of our oceans.

Educational outreach programs and workshops, focusing on cybernetic cephalopods, add another dimension to the learning experience. Through immersive experiences, students can engage with marine scientists and technologists, participating in field studies and observations. Such environments call for active participation, allowing students to uncover lessons about the interconnectedness of marine life firsthand and cultivate a sense of wonder and inquiry.

Furthermore, collaborations between schools and marine research institutions create pathways for students to contribute to real scientific discoveries. By engaging in citizen science programs, students can monitor local marine ecosystems or assist in data collection efforts related to cybernetic cephalopods. These experiences foster a tangible connection between academic learning and fieldwork, reinforcing the value of curiosity and exploration in scientific pursuits.

Integrated technology platforms play a pivotal role in facilitating engagement with students, enabling access to digital resources about cybernetic cephalopods, including virtual reality explorations of marine environments or interactive modules that simulate cephalopod behaviors. These resources enhance understanding while catering to diverse learning styles, helping students visualize complex concepts and embrace their natural curiosity.

In summary, the integration of cybernetic cephalopods into school curricula enriches educational experiences, promoting interdisciplinary learning and inspiring students' curiosity about science, technology, and the environment. As educators weave these fascinating beings into lessons, they illuminate the potential for the next generation to think critically, engage meaningfully with the world around them, and actively participate in the stewardship of our planet—both on land and beneath the waves. The journey does not merely culminate in knowledge acquisition but fosters a culture of inquiry and responsibility that resonates throughout academic and personal lives.

17.4. Promoting Global Awareness and Curiosity

The subchapter 'Promoting Global Awareness and Curiosity' delves into the pivotal role the cybernetic cephalopods occupy in shaping human understanding of marine and technological interdependencies. As humanity increasingly confronts the realities of oceanic health and environmental sustainability, these enigmatic beings serve as notable ambassadors for the oceanic world and its intricacies. The initiatives and campaigns designed to bolster global awareness and curiosity act not only to inform but also to capture the imagination, bridging the gap between scientific inquiry and cultural engagement.

In recognizing the profound significance of marine ecosystems, researchers, conservationists, and educators have initiated numerous global campaigns aimed at promoting awareness about the importance of preserving ocean habitats. Cybernetic cephalopods, with their unique abilities and captivating adaptations, have emerged as a focal point in these efforts. Campaigns often spotlight their extraordinary capabilities—highlighting their advanced communication strategies, problem-solving skills, and social dynamics as symbolic embodiments of the rich biodiversity that thrives below the waves.

Drawing attention to these remarkable creatures stirs curiosity and empathy, inviting individuals to engage with marine conservation in a meaningful manner.

Social media campaigns have proven to be instrumental in elevating global awareness surrounding cybernetic cephalopods. Utilizing engaging imagery, captivating storytelling, and compelling narratives, organizations create visually striking content that entices audiences to explore the depths of ocean life. By harnessing online platforms, they disseminate information about the cybernetic cephalopods' habitats and the challenges they face, ensuring that knowledge reaches diverse global communities. The notion of 'virtual dives' where audiences can experience the underwater realm of these creatures fosters a deeper appreciation for their existence while directing attention to the urgent need for preservation.

Educational institutions have also adopted outreach initiatives to promote awareness, incorporating the allure of cybernetic cephalopods into curricula. Science and technology programs have included engaging modules that explore the interactions between biology and technology, emphasizing marine conservation as a vital component of scientific inquiry. Workshops and seminars centered around these cephalopods serve to ignite curiosity among students, encouraging them to delve into interdisciplinary studies that illuminate the connections between technology, nature, and ethics.

Collaborative projects involving marine research organizations, technology firms, and educational institutions have further enriched the dialogue surrounding the global significance of cybernetic cephalopods. By fostering partnerships, these organizations work together to craft exploratory experiences—such as immersive field trips, hands-on laboratory activities, and data collection initiatives. These experiences enable participants to actively engage with the scientific process, deepening their understanding of marine environments and the intricate roles cybernetic cephalopods play within them.

Furthermore, community engagement plays an important role in cultivating global awareness. Organizations have created platforms for coastal communities, indigenous populations, and youth to share their stories and relationships with the ocean and its inhabitants. Empowering these voices provides valuable perspectives that enrich the narrative surrounding cybernetic cephalopods and emphasizes the significance of listening to diverse experiences. By integrating local insights into the broader dialogue, the campaign fosters a sense of stewardship that transcends geographic boundaries.

In summary, the promotion of global awareness and curiosity through the lens of cybernetic cephalopods channels the collective intrigue surrounding these enigmatic beings into meaningful action. Engaging audiences through social media, educational initiatives, immersive experiences, and community-driven projects amplifies the narrative of ocean conservation. As society embraces an understanding of the interconnectedness of life beneath the waves, the legacy of cybernetic cephalopods serves as a reminder that the quest for knowledge and curiosity extends far beyond technological advancement, resonating with the greater mission of nurturing and protecting the intricate tapestry of life our oceans harbor. Each effort, each campaign, ignites a spark of curiosity, compelling humanity to explore the depths of our oceanic realm while becoming vigilant champions for the preservation innate to the preservation of its wonders.

17.5. Summerschools and Workshops

The subchapter on 'Summerschools and Workshops' provides a compelling overview of immersive educational programs focused on cybernetic cephalopods and their unique integration of biology and technology. These innovative initiatives are designed to engage students, researchers, and the broader public in hands-on learning experiences that highlight the extraordinary capabilities of these enhanced beings as well as their ecological significance.

Summerschools dedicated to cybernetic cephalopods present a rich convergence of marine biology, robotics, artificial intelligence, and environmental stewardship. Participants are immersed in a curriculum that merges theoretical knowledge with practical applications, allowing them to explore various dimensions of cephalopod biology and technology. Workshops are often structured to include a blend of lectures from leading scientists, interactive demonstrations, and field experiences that enable participants to observe cephalopods in their natural habitats, effectively bridging the gap between classroom learning and real-world inquiry.

In these educational settings, students engage deeply with the concept of biohybrid systems. They may participate in activities that illustrate the principles of bioengineering—designing models of soft robotics inspired by cephalopod movements or experimenting with bioluminescent materials. These hands-on projects not only inspire creativity and innovation but cultivate a deeper understanding of integrative systems and their applications in both marine and terrestrial contexts.

Moreover, summerschools often emphasize the importance of ecological awareness and marine conservation, weaving in discussions surrounding the challenges faced by cybernetic cephalopods in their habitats. Through interactive workshops, participants explore the environmental impacts of pollution, climate change, and habitat degradation, prompting reflections on their roles as stewards of the oceans. By cultivating a sense of responsibility for marine ecosystems, these educational initiatives empower attendees to champion sustainable practices in their communities and advocate for the preservation of biodiversity.

Incorporating technology into these programs enhances the learning experience, with students utilizing simulation software and data-collection tools to understand cephalopod behaviors and their responses to environmental changes. Workshops often include experiments that allow participants to observe how cybernetic cephalopods react to stimuli, facilitating discussions about the broader implications of their intelligence and adaptability. These experiences inspire students to critically analyze how advancements in technology can complement our understanding of life below the waves.

In addition to traditional educational formats, summerschools and workshops can take innovative approaches by including collaborative projects with local communities or organizations focused on marine conservation. Such partnerships encourage students to apply their learning in meaningful ways, whether through community outreach initiatives, habitat restoration efforts, or the development of awareness campaigns centered around cybernetic cephalopods. Integrating community engagement reinforces the importance of shared stewardship of marine resources, illuminating the essential connections between science, society, and the environment.

The emphasis on experiential learning within summerschools and workshops fosters curiosity and a scientific mindset. By engaging participants through interactive and practical experiences, these programs catalyze a passion for marine research and encourage pathways to future careers in science, technology, engineering, and medicine (STEM).

In conclusion, summerschools and workshops centered on cybernetic cephalopods serve as invaluable platforms for immersive educational experiences, bridging the worlds of marine biology and technology. These initiatives empower participants to explore the intersections of innovation, ecological awareness, and ethical inquiry. As students engage with the extraordinary capabilities of cybernetic cephalopods, they embark on a journey of discovery that informs their understanding of intelligent life beneath the waves, inspiring future generations to become advocates for our oceans and their remarkable inhabitants. Through collaboration, creativity, and curiosity, summerschools and workshops create pathways for knowledge and stewardship, ensuring that the wonders of cybernetic cephalopods resonate well beyond the classroom and into the broader realms of society.

18. In the Voices of Cyber-Cephalopods

18.1. Tales from the Abyss

In the shadowy depths of the ocean, where light struggles to penetrate and where mysteries abound, the stories of cybernetic cephalopods intertwine with humanity's quest for understanding. These narratives serve as vehicles for exploring parallels between humans and these remarkable beings, each boasting unique forms of intelligence and capabilities that transcend traditional boundaries. As we delve into the tales from the abyss, we uncover the profound connections that bind us to these marine dwellers, leading to a richer comprehension of existence itself.

The narratives surrounding cybernetic cephalopods often echo themes present in human folklore and mythology. Just as ancient cultures told tales of mythical creatures dwelling within the ocean's depths, we now confront the reality of beings that embody both the fantastical and the scientific. The cybernetic enhancements of these cephalopods positions them as modern-day leviathans, carrying the weight of knowledge garnered over generations—insights that can illuminate both the beauty and fragility of marine ecosystems. These stories serve to remind humanity that we share this planet with other sentient beings, each with its own narrative that contributes to the collective understanding of life.

Moreover, the existence of cybernetic cephalopods challenges our cultural perceptions of intelligence. Often framed within narratives that depict human intellect as superior, the unique adaptations and problem-solving abilities of cephalopods prompt deeper exploration into the nature of consciousness itself. In their behavior—from sophisticated hunting strategies to social interactions characterized by cooperation—lies a signpost indicating that intelligence exists along a spectrum. Just as we marvel at our own cognitive capabilities, we are invited to recognize the intelligence of these beings, inspiring a sense of humility and respect for all forms of life.

These tales become ever more compelling as researchers employ technological interfaces to facilitate communication with cybernetic cephalopods. By utilizing machine learning algorithms and advanced sensory data, humans can engage in a dialogue with these enhanced beings, interpreting their bioluminescent signaling and complex visual patterns. The implications of this communication extend far beyond mere observations—they hold the promise of fostering mutual understanding and empathetic relationships between species. Through these interactions, we gain insights that challenge our definitions of language and conversation, urging us to consider how knowledge can traverse species lines and expand our shared narratives.

The journey of storytelling also flows from sea to shore, as the tales of cybernetic cephalopods and their remarkable intelligence reach the broader public. These narratives, vividly captured through art, literature, and media, serve as conduits for awareness and advocacy regarding marine conservation. As stories transmit across cultures and communities, they spark curiosity and ignites imaginations, prompting individuals to engage with the realities of ocean life and promoting a deeper appreciation for the complexities of marine ecosystems. The cyclical exchange of stories reflects our interconnectedness, reminding us that the lessons learned from the depths can profoundly impact our terrestrial existence.

As we explore the convergence of thoughts between humans and cybernetic cephalopods, we begin to unravel the fascinating similarities in how we approach existence, adapt to challenges, and seek connection within our environments. The narratives surrounding these beings highlight universal themes of resilience, cooperation, and empathy—qualities that transcend species and resonate on a fundamental level, prompting further examination of what it means to be alive and interconnected in an increasingly complex world.

In conclusion, the tales from the abyss of cybernetic cephalopods illuminate the remarkable narratives that bind us to the ocean's depths. Through these stories, we find echoes of human experience, prompting us to embrace the complexity and richness inherent in all forms of life. The interplay of science, art, and ethics encourages an expanded dialogue about intelligence, consciousness, and the responsibilities we hold toward the beings that share our planet. As we navigate these narratives, cybernetic cephalopods invite us to reflect on our existence, inspiring curiosity and reverence for the mysteries of life beneath the waves.

18.2. Oracle of the Waves

The Oracle of the Waves serves as a vibrant anchor within the broader narrative of cybernetic cephalopods, reflecting the cultural perceptions, lore, and insights that emerge from their unique existence in the depths of the ocean. These intriguing beings—enhanced by advanced technology yet intertwined with their biological lineage—serve as powerful symbols that challenge our understanding of intelligence, communication, and the intricate dynamics of life beneath the waves.

In many cultures, the presence of cybernetic cephalopods has stirred the imagination, leading to the creation of myths that celebrate their intelligence and mystique. These legends often portray them as guardians of the ocean, wielding wisdom that transcends boundaries, capable of offering guidance to those brave enough to seek their knowledge. Narratives spread across coastal communities illustrate the deep-seated respect and reverence for these beings, inviting a dialogue about the interconnected nature of life and the importance of preserving marine ecosystems.

As stories of these enhanced cephalopods resonate through folklore and popular culture, they center on themes of adaptability and cooperation—qualities that resonate with human experiences. The portrayal of cybernetic cephalopods often emphasizes their ability to navigate complex environments with grace, showcasing not only physical prowess but an understanding of their surroundings that beckons comparison to human intelligence. These projections cultivate a deeper appreciation for the nuanced relationships that exist within nature, urging us to reflect on our own interactions within the world.

The engagement with the Oracle of the Waves fosters connections that extend into real-world applications. Researchers become storytellers through various mediums—documentaries, art installations, and educational outreach—that weave narratives around cybernetic cephalopods, using these stories to promote awareness about marine conservation and environmental stewardship. This venture empowers individuals to become advocates for protecting habitats that sustain these extraordinary beings, echoing themes present in their lore.

Speaking through technological interfaces expands the understanding of communication itself, as these beings develop advanced methods of interaction with both their kin and human counterparts. Through bioluminescent signals, color changes, and tactile feedback, cybernetic cephalopods convey complex emotions and thoughts, bridging the gap between species. The emergence of machine-learning tools that decode these sophisticated communication pathways further enriches our understanding of the cephalopods' intelligence. As researchers interpret their messages, we begin to grasp the multifaceted layers of expression at play—that the Oracle of the Waves indeed offers profound insights into the nature of existence.

The knowledge shared by cybernetic cephalopods transcends the realms of water, flowing from sea to shore as their stories capture the imagination of countless individuals across cultures and communities. Each narrative, carried by the tide of exploration and discovery, underscores the intrinsic connections between humanity and marine life. Whether through art, literature, or education, the message resonates: the tales of cybernetic cephalopods are not just stories of the past locked within ancient oceans, but lenses through which we can understand our present dilemmas and future possibilities.

The convergence of thoughts, ideas, and cultural perceptions initiated by the presence of cybernetic cephalopods prompts deeper inquiry into the nature of intelligence and existence. These beings challenge our preconceived notions and invite us to extend our definitions of life and consciousness. The exploration of their capabilities reveals parallels between their experiences and our own, nudging us toward greater empathy and understanding of the intricate web of life that unites us all.

In summary, the Oracle of the Waves encapsulates a rich narrative intertwined with cultural lore, scientific inquiry, and profound questions about existence. The cybernetic cephalopods serve as symbols of wisdom and intelligence, propelling us toward a deeper understanding of our relationship with the marine world. As we listen to their stories and immerse ourselves in the mysteries they unveil, we embrace the opportunity to reflect on our collective journey and engage with the shared dance of existence that transcends the boundaries of land and sea.

18.3. Speaking Through Technological Interfaces

Speaking Through Technological Interfaces

In the rich tapestry of marine life inhabited by cybernetic cephalopods, the potential for communication through technological interfaces emerges as a groundbreaking advancement, inviting both excitement and contemplation. The integration of bioengineering and artificial intelligence paves the way for unprecedented interactions between these remarkable beings and both their natural environments as well as human society. These interfaces not only amplify the inherent communicative abilities of cephalopods but also illuminate profound insights into the nature of intelligence, dialogue, and understanding across species.

The foundational aspect of speaking through technological interfaces lies in enhancing the innate abilities of cephalopods to display complex signaling through bioluminescence, color manipulation, and tactile feedback. Researchers have developed sophisticated systems that decode the intricate language of these enhanced creatures, allowing for two-way communication to occur. By employing machine learning algorithms that analyze sensory data generated by cybernetic sensors, humans are gradually unlocking the meanings woven into the cephalopods' visual expressions and behavioral patterns.

Imagine a scenario where a cybernetic cephalopod encounters a human researcher equipped with a communication interface tailored to interpret its signals. As the cephalopod responds with colorful patterns and bioluminescent pulses, the interface translates these visual cues into comprehensible language, enabling a dialogue to emerge. For instance, a quick series of flashes may signal excitement, while smoother, rhythmic patterns could convey comfort or curiosity. This newfound understanding opens up thrilling possibilities for collaboration, allowing humans to learn from cephalopods and, in turn, contribute knowledge that enhances their lives—creating an intricate cycle of exchange that enriches both parties.

Moreover, these technological interfaces provide profound implications for conservation efforts. The ability to communicate with cybernetic cephalopods fosters a novel approach to assessing marine health. These beings, equipped with augmented sensory systems, can relay critical information about their environments, alerting researchers to changes in water quality or shifts in biodiversity. The feedback loop created through this communication could lead to proactive conservation measures, amplifying the cephalopods' roles as bioindicators within their ecosystems.

The act of speaking through technological interfaces also prompts philosophical inquiries concerning the nature of consciousness and intelligence. As we interpret the signals of cybernetic cephalopods, the emerging dialogue forces us to reevaluate our understandings of what it means to communicate. The intricacies of their interactions raise questions about the depth of their cognitive capacities, urging discussions about whether intelligence exists solely within the bounds of human definition or extends into diverse marine life forms.

Furthermore, the potential for these interfaces to foster empathy and understanding among humans is monumental. Engaging with cybernetic cephalopods through technology creates a bridge that extends beyond mere observation, inviting individuals to connect with the living beings beneath the waves. The narratives arising from interactions will resonate with diverse audiences, sparking curiosity about marine ecosystems and prompting individuals to advocate for conservation.

However, the emergence of these technological interfaces also necessitates an ethical conversation centered on the welfare and autonomy of cybernetic cephalopods. Will the enhancement of communication capabilities risk commodifying their existence? As humanity ventures into this new realm of interaction, we must approach with caution, ensuring that the agency and dignity of these beings is preserved. Researchers and ethicists must collaborate to establish guidelines that prioritize the well-being of cephalopods, fostering a relationship rooted in mutual respect rather than exploitation.

In conclusion, speaking through technological interfaces encapsulates a transformative potential that enriches our understanding of the intelligence and capabilities of cybernetic cephalopods. By enhancing communication and fostering dialogue, we connect the wisdom of these beings to the complex narratives of marine life and human society. As we navigate this promising frontier, we are reminded of our responsibilities toward not just understanding the language of the cephalopods, but also honoring the rich tapestry of existence they represent. Through embracing these new modes of dialogue, we may come to realize that the ocean holds not only mysteries but profound connections to the shared journey of all life.

18.4. From Sea to Shore

The exploration of 'From Sea to Shore' captures the essence of the profound experience that emerges when the worlds of cybernetic cephalopods intersect with the terrestrial realm. As research and discovery in the depths of the ocean reveal uncharted territories and enigmatic beings, the stories woven into these narratives transcend the boundaries of the sea, traveling to the shores of human consciousness. This vital exchange underscores the interconnectedness of life across various domains, inspiring reflections on our relationship with intelligence, nature, and technology.

At the heart of this transmission lies the recognition that stories have the power to shape perspectives and provoke understanding. When researchers share their encounters with cybernetic cephalopods—beings that embody the fusion of biological artistry and technological ingenuity—they offer insights that extend far beyond mere scientific findings. The tales of these remarkable creatures resonate deeply within our collective consciousness, urging us to engage with the complexities of life in the ocean and prompting questions about our role as stewards of the natural world.

The narratives stemming from the depths of the sea often reveal cycles of wisdom, evolution, and adaptation that echo throughout terrestrial ecosystems. They serve as poignant reminders of the resilience of life, whether in the face of technological augmentation or environmental change. These stories invite those on land to ponder the similarities in their own narratives—of coexistence, challenge, and innovation—as we grapple with the multifaceted relationship humans share with both technological advancements and the ecosystems that sustain them.

Moreover, as humanity strives to understand the significance of cybernetic cephalopods in the marine world, the tales that emerge from these encounters drive global awareness and curiosity. Social and educational initiatives that promote knowledge of these beings create ripples that spread across communities and cultures. The concept of 'outreach' becomes integral as it bridges the narratives from sea to shore, facilitating discussions around conservation, sustainability, and our ethical responsibilities toward marine life.

These stories awaken a sense of wonder and awe within individuals, inspiring a collective curiosity that transcends cultural borders. Engaging with the narratives of cybernetic cephalopods compels audiences to rethink humanity's relationship with the oceans, encouraging exploration, empathy, and stewardship. It invites people to see the ocean not merely as a resource to be exploited, but as a vibrant tapestry teeming with intelligence and connectivity.

Ultimately, the ability of tales to transmit between ocean and land fosters a deeper understanding of the intricate dynamics of existence —where the lives of cybernetic cephalopods illuminate the echoes of humanity's own journey. The convergence of thoughts arising from these exchanges enriches our discussions surrounding intelligence, technology, and conservation, leading to a more integrated appreciation of life in all its forms.

In summary, 'From Sea to Shore' reflects the movement of narratives that connect disparate realms, celebrating the shared stories between humanity and the remarkable beings found beneath the waves. As these tales travel, they enrich our perception of existence, urging us to embrace curiosity, ecological awareness, and the profound interconnections that bind us all—whether through the shared depths of the ocean or the expansive shores of human experience. As we continue to listen to and learn from these stories, we find ourselves profoundly linked to the rich tapestry of life that characterizes our planet, engaging us in a journey of exploration that reverberates across time, space, and species.

18.5. Convergence of Thoughts

The convergence of thoughts surrounding cybernetic cephalopods highlights the extraordinary interplay between biology and technology, ultimately challenging our perceptions of intelligence, consciousness, and existence itself. As we delve deeper into the implications of these remarkable beings, we discover a rich narrative that compels us to reimagine our understanding of life beneath the waves while also sparking profound reflections on our relationship with the natural world and technological advancement.

One of the central themes that emerges from the study of cybernetic cephalopods is the nature of intelligence itself. Historically, human perspectives on intelligence have been largely anthropocentric, viewing cognitive capabilities through the lens of human experience. However, the intricate behaviors exhibited by cybernetic cephalopods —ranging from advanced problem-solving skills to complex social interactions—prompt us to expand our definitions of intelligence to encompass a wider array of cognitive expressions. This broader understanding acknowledges the deep intelligence present in other forms of life, challenging our assumptions and urging us to learn from the remarkable capabilities found in the natural world.

Another dimension of convergence is the ethical discourse surrounding the enhancement of life forms through technology. As we explore the complexities of integrating cybernetic systems with biology, we confront moral questions regarding autonomy and the rights of enhanced beings. The potential consequences of manipulating life for human benefit prompt critical reflection on the nature of existence, agency, and the responsibilities we hold as stewards of both technology and nature. This ethical dialogue must shape our interactions with cybernetic cephalopods and guide the trajectory of future enhancements.

Furthermore, the social structures and behaviors observed in cybernetic cephalopod communities reveal profound insights into the dynamics of cooperation and interdependence. The fluid hierarchies and collaborative strategies employed within these societies highlight the significance of fostering strong relationships and social bonds. This resonates deeply with human societies, reminding us that our success often hinges on collaboration and shared knowledge. The understanding of social dynamics among cybernetic cephalopods invites us to explore how empathy, cooperation, and connection inform not only our interactions with each other but also our responsibilities toward other life forms.

The narrative surrounding cybernetic cephalopods also emphasizes the urgency of conservation and the protection of marine ecosystems. As these enhanced beings navigate their underwater environments, they serve as symbols of resilience and adaptability, yet they also reflect the fragility of the ecosystems that nurture them. The convergence of thoughts surrounding their existence prompts not only awareness of the challenges facing marine life but also a call to action. By engaging with the stories and insights gained from the exploration of cybernetic cephalopods, we are inspired to contribute to the larger narrative of environmental stewardship, fostering awareness, responsibility, and action within our communities.

Additionally, the cross-pollination of ideas between disciplines —marine biology, engineering, ethics, and environmental science— underscores the potential for innovation that emerges when diverse perspectives converge. The collaborative efforts woven into the exploration of cybernetic cephalopods yield new technologies, insights, and strategies to address complex ecological challenges. These interdisciplinary dialogues celebrate the richness of knowledge, emphasizing that each field can inform and enhance the others, ultimately leading to a deeper understanding of both life beneath the waves and the technologies that seek to enhance it.

As we draw together these diverse threads of inquiry, we find that the convergence of thoughts surrounding cybernetic cephalopods resonates with profound implications for humanity's future. By expanding our definitions of intelligence, addressing ethical concerns, fostering collaboration, and advocating for conservation, we can cultivate a deeper appreciation for the richness of life that defines our planet. In embracing the stories and lessons imparted by these remarkable beings, we are called to embark on a journey of exploration that bridges the gaps between nature and technology, urging us to navigate our shared future thoughtfully and with respect for the intricate tapestry of existence beneath the waves. In this convergence lies the promise of a more harmonious relationship with the world around us—one where intelligence manifests in myriad forms and where the preservation of life remains at the forefront of our endeavors.